E-Go - Ego Distancing Through Mindfulness, Emotional Intelligence and the Language of Love

by Taite Adams

Rapid   Response   Press
1730 Lighthouse Terr. S., Suite 12
So   Pasadena,   FL   33707
www.rapidresponsepress.com
Ordering   Information:
Quantity sales. Special discounts are available on quantity purchases by corporations, associations, and others. For details, contact the publisher   at   the   address   above.
Orders by U.S. trade bookstores and wholesalers. Please contact Rapid Response Press: Tel: (866) 983-3025; Fax: (855) 877-4736 or visit www. rapidresponsepress.com.
Printed in the United States of America
Publisher's   Cataloging-in-Publication   data
Adams,   Taite.
A title of a book : a subtitle of the same book / Taite Adams.
p.   cm.
ISBN   978-0-9907674-1-1
1. The main category of the book —Self-Help —General category. 2. Another subject category —Self-Help - Spiritual. 3. More categories —Self-Help - Personal Growth.

First Edition
==================

Limit of Liability/Disclaimer of Warranty

================

Disclaimer

===================

Medical Disclaimer

The information contained in this book is not intended to serve as a replacement for professional medical advice. Any use of the information in this book is at the reader's discretion. The author and publisher specifically disclaim any and all liability arising directly or indirectly from the use or application of any information contained in this book. A health care professional should be consulted regarding your specific situation.

To my Son - Our long talks always leave my heart enriched and my smile brighter;

To Mom & Dad - My best ideas about life and love came from you;

To my Love - I count you at the top of my many blessings daily. Your love and support is a constant reminder that my life is, indeed, perfect.

See http://www.TaiteAdams.com for more info

Taite Adams

Table of Contents

Preface

I count him braver who overcomes his desires than him who conquers his enemies; for the hardest victory is over self. - Aristotle

When I was a bit younger, if anyone were to tell me that I would later be writing a book about ego, I'd have probably grinned at them and said, "You're damn right I will and it will be a Best Seller!". I equated ego in those days only with self-confidence and, to me, the more of it that I had, the better. Any sign of humility coming from me was false and usually in the form of humblebragging or admitting a mistake to the detriment of someone else. I really didn't get it.

I allowed my ego to run roughshod over my life, and that of those closest to me, for many years. I say "I allowed" although I'm not really sure that this is the most accurate depiction of went on. The truth is that I had no idea what was controlling me for so long. I only knew that I was defining myself based upon external factors, feeling separate from everyone and everything and self-medicating to get past feelings of inadequacy.

Despite the fact that I was brought up in a loving home with kind parents, I know now that ideas instilled at an early age formed a belief system that was not serving me well in this life. Whether it be the era, location or manner of my upbringing, it doesn't really matter. Rigid ideas and beliefs about life, love, success and even God turned me into someone who was wound up tighter than a top and who became desperate for relief.

As I began to learn more about myself, my eyes were opened to the possibilities for so much more. I became aware that this thing called ego, shaped early in life, was directing a lot of my thoughts and behaviors - behaviors in relationships, in my career, and even behaviors that were having an effect on my physical and mental health. By taking the time to understand what some of my subconscious belief systems were, I could then set about making changes to those underlying beliefs.

Some on self-help quests are looking for guidance to "kill the ego". It is widely understood in most circles that this simply isn't possible. Ego is a part of self that is essential for existence. It is the extent to which ego drives thoughts and behaviors that is the key. What ego does, when it is dominant, is keeps you from realizing your true nature in this world. Ego distancing, therefore, will allow you to plug into something much bigger than you ever dreamed possible. This is what I have found to be true.

Taite Adams

Introduction

You are a beautiful soul hidden by the trench coat of the ego. - Mike Dolan

Regardless of when you think your ego ideas were developed, it is widely agreed upon that they were pretty early in life. Ideas about what is right and wrong, the things that we should be striving for, prejudices, and the like are generally formed by adolescence. These ideas come from any number of sources. I know that when I first saw Charlie's Angel's at the tender age of 6, I decided right then and there that I was going to grow up and become a bad ass female detective with a gun. I held onto that idea for many years until the more conservative values instilled by family won out and I went to work in the insurance field. Why do this? Ego says we are defined by our success.

The way that we relate to each other as human beings and the things that we place value on have continued to change over time, especially with advances in technology. Instead of spending time with friends and family, we text them or "like" something they've posted online. Ego plays a big role here as social media makes it easier and easier to get mired in self - posting constant updates and monitoring who comments on or "likes" them, checking to see which friends are out on the town without you, and keeping tabs on people you don't even like. Why do we do this? Ego says it matters what other people think about us.

Ego sends a lot of messages through the sub-conscious that do not serve our true nature, even a little bit. If the need to be right or to feel superior to others is an on-going pull, you are not alone. If you identify based upon achievements, possessions or what others think of

xv

you, consider yourself lucky to recognize it and own it. These sorts of beliefs are of the ego and create havoc in all areas of people's lives - not the least being in relationships, career and even health. Ego distancing is the answer and it's not as difficult as it sounds.

Unfortunately, ego distancing doesn't happen just by wishing it to be so. It does require a change in attitudes and, more importantly, the actual taking of some action. In this book there are a lot of action items listed in each section so that you can be a participant in your transformation. Consistent action is one sure way to change belief systems. Others are provided as well. Mindfulness, emotional intelligence and love are steady themes repeated throughout.

Mindfulness, oftentimes referred to as "staying present", means maintaining a moment-by-moment awareness of your thoughts, feelings and surroundings. Ego never wants you to be in the present moment so learning to practice mindfulness is a sure-fire method of ego distancing. There are many ways to help you do this, and even benefits listed, as we move forward.

Emotional Intelligence (EQ) has become a self-help catch phrase in recent years and it does have implications for ego identification and ego distancing. In fact, the first category of emotional intelligence is self-awareness. If you are unable to get to a place of recognizing emotions, their source and their effects, you'll have little chance in ever controlling them. I believe that all of the factors of EQ are important in ego-distancing to an extent, yet I think that the "social skills" factor can tend to get twisted by some. I don't believe that we have the ability to control another person's emotions, only to influence by always being kind and loving.

The language of love is a theme that I hope runs through every page of this book. Ego doesn't want us to be loving, forgiving and kind to each other or even to ourselves. We talk about the surest way to distance from ego and our illusions of separation by speaking the language of love.

All learning has an emotional base. - Plato

Part I - The Essentials of the Ego

What is Ego?

Through pride we are ever deceiving ourselves. But deep down below the surface of the average conscience a still, small voice says to us, something is out of tune. - Carl Jung

If you asked ten people the question "What is Ego?", you'd likely wind up with ten different answers. Several may be similar in some regards but we all tend to have our own ideas about what ego is and isn't and these are very personal, as they should be. In my studies of all things "ego", I have run across some very interesting theories, many I agree with and can related to my own experiences, while others are a bit more difficult to grasp. That's not to say that they don't hold weight. Some theorists, such as Freud, just take a few extra cups of coffee or an extra twenty minutes in the meditation chair to prepare for. Let's take a look at a few of these ideas about ego, starting with the heavy lifting first.

Freud's Definition of Ego

The mind is like an iceberg, it floats with one-seventh of its bulk above water. - Sigmund Freud

Sigmund Freud is inarguably one of the most influential thinkers of the twentieth century and has been called Psychology's most famous figure. His work and theories have helped to shape how we look at sexuality, childhood, and personality in several different ways. Either other theorists have used these ideas to expand on their own theories or have used them to develop new theories that debunk them completely. Regardless, when we hear the word "ego", many people jump to Freud's definition first and this bears some examination.

Freud first discussed the ego in his model of the human psyche in his 1920 essay *Beyond the Pleasure Principle* and later elaborated upon it in *The Ego and the Id*, published in 1923. According to Freud's theory of personality, the personality is composed of three elements. These three elements - known as the Id, the Ego, and the Superego - work together to create complex human behaviors.

E-Go

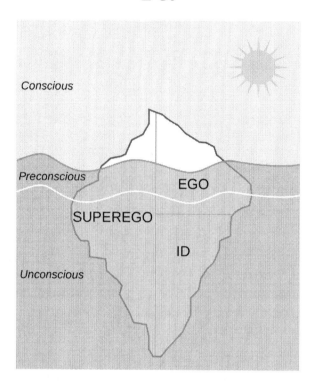

Taite Adams

The Id

Where Id was, there ego shall be. - Sigmund Freud

The only component to our personality that is present at birth, the Id allows us to get our basic needs met. Freud ties the Id back to the Pleasure Principle in that the Id is only looking for instant gratification and cares nothing about reality or anyone else's needs or feelings. For example, if a baby were hungry, they would cry until that need was satisfied. This is an important survival element early in life yet can become troublesome if it is the driving force as we get older.

You know what it feels like when you desire something very deeply? It could be another person, a job promotion, a new car or something else. There is a physical and psychological component at work when this desire kicks in and Freud ties this primal desire back to the Id. Is this a bad thing? Not always. Desire as a motivator for achievement and even for survival isn't a bad thing. It's when desire drives us to grab more than our share or harm others that issues arise. This is where Freud's Ego comes in.

Towards the outside, at any rate, the ego seems to maintain clear and sharp lines of demarcation. There is only one state — admittedly an unusual state, but not one that can be stigmatized as pathological — in which it does not do this. At the height of being in love the boundary between ego and object threatens to melt away. Against all the evidence of his senses, a man who is in love declares that "I" and "you" are one, and is prepared to behave as if it were a fact. - Sigmund Freud

The Ego

The ego represents what we call reason and sanity, in contrast to the id which contains the passions. - Sigmund Freud

While the Id operates primarily on what Freud calls The Pleasure Principle, the Ego operates on what is called the reality principle. This means that the ego works to satisfy those many desires of the Id while taking into account the world around it and what is socially appropriate. Once a child is a few years old, they usually have learned that instant gratification in all instances is not going to happen and is oftentimes not the best idea.

The ego takes hold by beginning to act as an intervention between demanding that our desires be fulfilled immediately to the appropriate suppression of urges or strategy building. Urges can be suppressed by using mental delay tactics that allow the person to put off satisfaction for a period time by calling up mental images. Strategy building is something different altogether. Ego can also facilitate the planning and mapping out of just how said urge is going to be fulfilled at some point in the very near future. This has endless implications for negative outcomes.

It is easy to see that the ego is that part of the id which has been modified by the direct influence of the external world. - Sigmund Freud

The Superego

It is impossible to escape the impression that people commonly use false standards of measurement — that they seek power, success and wealth for themselves and admire them in others, and that they underestimate what is of true value in life. - Sigmund Freud

The Superego, according to Freud, is the last to develop because it is based upon our internalized moral standards and ideals. These are our truths that we've developed from parents, caregivers and society that form our sense of values and drive the way that we label things as "right and wrong". This allows us to make judgments and these judgments work to civilize our behavior with regards to getting our wants and needs met.

The Superego is made up of two components: the ego ideal and the conscience. The ego ideals are our internal standards for good behaviors. When we keep to these standards, or rules, we tend to feel a sense of pride and value. The conscience is internal information about what is "bad" when it comes to behavior. Going against conscience can lead to feelings of guilt and remorse and can oftentimes result in external consequences.

The ego is not master in its own house. - Sigmund Freud

The Dance

The poor ego has a still harder time of it; it has to serve three harsh masters, and it has to do its best to reconcile the claims and demands of all three... The three tyrants are the external world, the superego, and the id. - Sigmund Freud

Freud sees these three as frequently competing, or dueling, forces that can often create conflict. He maintains that the key to a healthy personality is the balance between the three. If the Id is too strong, a person is ruled by self-gratification. If the superego is too strong, a person may be too rigid with their unbending morals and judgments of the outside world.

What is most interesting are his notions about the subconscious and conscious, stating that the Ego is really the only one of the three that is fully conscious. In other words, what you perceive as "You", Freud would call your Ego self. As the Ego operates on the reality principle, you are taking the subconscious desires of the Id, along with your superego's desire for you to be a good person and your ego is interpreting those into real actions.

While all very deep, and somewhat complex, Freud's ideas about personality do make a lot of sense to me. It is clear that we are born with only the want and need to fill our basic desires, generally the survival instinct. Beyond that, what we know individually about what is socially acceptable and the forming of values is taught and developed over time. These lessons formulate how we interact with the world around us and with each other. All of these have massive implications for the ego. Yet, taken a step further, there are some built in mechanisms for self deception that ego makes steady use of in any assortment of circumstances.

Being entirely honest with oneself is a good exercise. - Sigmund Freud

Taite Adams

Ego Defense Mechanisms

I was always looking outside myself for strength and confidence, but it comes from within. It is there all the time. - Anna Freud

Sigmund Freud reveals interesting theories about the ego and the various internal conflicts that it can create. However, it was his daughter, Anna Freud, who introduced the principle of inner mechanisms that defend the ego in her 1936 book "The Ego and the Mechanisms of Defense". These defense mechanisms are in place in order to lesson tension and anxiety brought on by conflicts or other such problems in life, whether real or imagined. Defense mechanisms operate at an unconscious level to protect the ego from negative feelings or consequences. There are many defense mechanisms but it is generally agreed that there are about nine major ones:

- Denial - By far the most common and one that can been found as a common thread running through some of the others. When denial is in play, a person simply refuses to recognize the truth, no matter how apparent. Examples of this are, "No. I'm a just a social drug user," or "He wouldn't have done that if I...".

- Repression - Actually the first mechanism discovered by Freud, it involves keeping disturbing ideas, desires, or memories in the subconscious so that guilt and shame is kept at bay. Unfortunately, it is rarely successful and often leads to increased anxiety. Examples of this are trying to forget childhood abuse or an accident in which you were at fault.

- Projection - A useful mechanism in many circumstances, this involves blame. An individual essentially throws their uncomfortable feelings, and usually insecurities, onto someone else. For example, you may feel competitive with a colleague and come to believe that they are incompetent, stupid and probably trying to undermine you behind your back.

- Intellectualization - A popular mechanism for those of us who like to think too much, this involves using analysis rather than emotion to deal with a situation that may otherwise cause you stress. For example, if your car is totaled and you are left without transportation, rather than sit and worry about the problem and its emotional consequences, you figure out on paper exactly what you can do and afford.

- Rationalization - Rationalization may sound like the prior mechanism but there is one key difference. This one is used to explain away and deflect negative feelings from some sort of bad behavior on your part. Rationalization is often used as a mechanism to remove guilt, shame or embarrassment from an indiscretion as well as a way to get rid of ongoing insecurities. For example, if you snapped at your co-worker and this is someone that you respect, you may explain it away by blaming your boss for provoking you earlier in the day.

- Displacement - Have you ever punched a wall when you were angry with someone? This is displacement. This mechanism dictates that you transfer your feelings, usually negatives ones like anger, away from their target and towards a more harmless victim. For example, you've had an awful day at school and that terrible professor has given you another "F" on a paper. Instead of telling the professor what you think of him, you come home and throw your backpack against the wall.

- Regression - Not the same as repression, regression involves reverting back to a childlike emotional state under situations of emotional stress. Things that we may not attribute to regression, really are. For example, road rage is really just an example of a childlike tantrum. Refusing to talk to people who have made you feel bad is another.

- Reaction Formation - Often misunderstood, reaction formation is really pretty straightforward. In an effort to protect themselves, sometimes people behave in a manner that is the opposite of their true feelings and desires. For example, being sweet as pie to a bitter enemy just to prove that you are "above that" or acting indifferent or even hateful to someone that you are really madly in love with.

- Sublimation - Sublimation is the defense mechanism that calls for acting out unacceptable impulses in a socially acceptable way. For example, someone that has a hidden need for violence decides to become a boxer or even a person who has an obsessive need for control that ends up being a successful entrepreneur.

Many of these defense mechanisms overlap and not all of them are bad. At times, defense mechanisms allow us to cope in the short-term with unpleasant emotions. However, in the long-term they don't serve anyone well as day-to-day tools. Two things hold true with ego defense mechanisms: they appear unconsciously and they tend to distort or falsify reality. It has been my experience that the longer one stays in full flight from reality, the more painful will be the landing.

So, is Freudian psychology the end all and be all when it comes to talking about the Ego? I sure hope not! While these ideas are interesting and have a lot of merit, they tend to be very complicated and I don't think that we need to dig that deep to get to the heart of the matter. Let's take a look at some other ways that ego controls our thoughts and behaviors. Then we'll break down the key components of healthy ego distancing, giving solid direction for lasting change in ideas and behavior.

Ego Defines Me

Very often a change of self is needed more than a change of scene. - A. C. Benson

How do you define yourself? Better yet, how would you define yourself if only given two words to do so? If you asked this question to a hundred different people, a majority would answer with external labels - things like: a nurse, a parent, an author, a homeowner. This isn't just supposition. My partner and I actually run quite a few large and diverse Facebook communities and put this question out there to the masses. The overwhelming majority of responses, the serious ones anyway, were ones in which people identified themselves based upon their career, possessions, or social status. This is where ego takes us naturally and quite easily.

Ego very much wants to make you think that your self worth is all about what you possess, what you've accomplished and who you know.

E-Go

Possessions - We are what we own.

Wealth consists not in having great possessions, but in having few wants. - *Epictetus*

Whether we are measuring our self worth based upon the things that we possess or comparing the things that we possess to those of our neighbor, this is all ego-based and you will never be satisfied. A person who drives a Ford Fiesta will become convinced that true happiness will be found only when he is behind the wheel of that BMW. Once the BMW is in the driveway, he just knows that he'd be much happier with a Porsche. And so on.

I have had a love-hate relationship with possessions all of my life. My parents were not wealthy by any means but, growing up an only child, I was spoiled to the core and usually ended up getting what I wanted if it was attainable. What I found over the years was that these "things" never brought lasting fulfillment. It didn't matter if it was cars, houses or the things that I'd fill those houses up with, it was never enough and I was always looking for that next material "fix" or conquest that would make me feel as if I had "arrived". Quite frankly, I never found it.

In a study published in 2012 titled "Life at Home in the Twenty-First Century," researchers at U.C.L.A. observed 32 middle-class Los Angeles families and found that all of the mothers' stress hormones spiked during the time they spent dealing with their belongings. Seventy-five percent of the families involved in the study couldn't park their cars in their garages because they were too jammed with things. Of course, these were important "things" at one time, things that they just had to have. Now they just take up space. Can you relate?

E-Go

There is no doubt that we love our possessions. Consider the simple numbers here with regards to the explosion of housing size over the past 60 years (U.S. Census Bureau Data). The average size of a new American home in 1950 was 983 square feet, with an average family size of 3.3 people; by 2011, the average new home was 2,480 square feet with just 2.6 people per household. So, we are taking up to three times more space per person than we did 60 years ago! Of course we are! We need room for all of our stuff. Apparently this still isn't enough space per person as evidenced by this nation's $22 billion private storage industry.

Do you know what is in all of those boxes that you refuse to let go of? The ones that you pay movers to cart from one location to the next? I found that I no longer did and wasn't getting much joy from the exercise anymore. What I eventually discovered was that I was looking in the wrong places, and at the wrong things, for fulfillment.

About ten years ago, I made a decision to move onto a boat and be a full time liveaboard. This necessitated my getting rid of nearly all of those worldly possessions that I had spent so many years accumulating and holding onto with an iron grip. I found this to be one of the most liberating experiences of my life. Things that I thought I could never live without, such as my massive book collection, were quickly forgotten as I became free of clutter and the need to accumulate even more.

The lesson for me became a very simple one. I wasn't an owner of things. They owned me. The more "things" I have, the more time I spend thinking about them, moving them around, fixing them, looking for them, or upgrading them. The less "things" I possess, the more time I have to spend with friends, family, meeting new people, and just enjoying life. This is true freedom and I'd prefer to define myself as someone who is free than as someone who lives in such and such neighborhood. I see nothing wrong with having nice things or driving a nice car, yet being defined by those things is another story and that is ego taking the wheel.

Career - We are what we do.

I've learned that making a 'living' is not the same thing as 'making a life'. - Maya
Angelou

Who are you? Overwhelmingly, people identify themselves based upon what they do for a living. I am a teacher, a lawyer, a nurse, a student, a bartender. While we may derive some our self worth based upon our career path and achievements, taking full credit for these things is where the trouble starts.

When we define ourselves based upon career position and achievements, we are generally doing several things. One is exercising a need to feel superior. If I announce that I am a lawyer, I am probably looking pretty smugly at everyone in the room who either isn't a lawyer, has been one for less time than I have, or who practices a field of law that I deem inferior to the one that I have mastered. The other issue with defining ourselves based on career is that we often want to take full credit for all of our achievements.

Well, who should take credit? Right? Actually, that is the key to this whole exercise because ego wants us to believe that we are separate from the Universal Source and from each other. So, if we are insisting that all of our achievements are "mine" and putting ourselves either above or below others when we look at professional achievements, this is ego shouting loud and clear.

Career advancement, and even educational achievements, used to be like a game to me. I became hooked when I got my first straight A report card late in high school. I loved the praise and attention that I received from this achievement and set out to earn more. I picked a major in college based on career path and the economy, not at all based on my interests. My first professional job was also something that wouldn't have blown your hair back on the excitement meter, but I was determined to be a top achiever. So much so that I was voted "Most Likely to Become CEO" by our training class.

While a cute award, I took that stuff seriously and competed with everyone about every little thing. I was the first to earn professional designations, to volunteer to head committees and to start towards an advanced degree. I'd become angry and resentful if passed over for a promotion and a prideful show-off if given any sort of accolades. At the age of 27, with an MBA, I finally got that job that I felt I really deserved and felt that I had "arrived" professionally. I was instantly miserable and lonelier than I ever have been in my life.

It was many years later before I really learned the lesson about identifying based on career and achievements. We can feel good about what we do for a living and our achievements but there are a few important caveats here. One is that we, alone, cannot take credit for all that we have become and achieved. We are merely vessels. Another is that our careers and achievements do not place us in a position of superiority or inferiority to anyone else - ever. Finally, we need to let go of the constant need and pull to have more. Have you ever heard this one - If you aren't happy with what you have, what makes you think you'd be happy with more? The ego is never satisfied. So, if you're not satisfied with what you have right now, consider what is driving you.

Reputation - We are what others think.

Who can know how much of his most inward life is made up of the thoughts he believes other men to have about him, until that fabric of opinion is threatened with ruin? - George Eliot

Are you of the mistaken belief that your reputation should have anything to do with what you think of yourself? Many people are. Quite the contrary. Our reputations are so out of our control that it's laughable how much time and effort so many of us put into to trying to "control" them. Reputation is the sum of the thoughts about us that reside in the minds of others.

Have you ever been, or do you know, someone who is so crippled with worry about what other people think that they either can't make a clear decision or run themselves in circles? Personal reputation management has never been one of my primary interests but I'd be lying if I said that I didn't care what other people thought of me at times, especially when those opinions may be negative. Funny how that works. What's key here is to recognize that everyone, including us, has their own agendas and are constantly interpreting the behavior of others through their own (distorted) lenses. This is a fact and people will place more value on certain things that you do or don't do and less value on others. If your actions aren't matching up to their particular value system at the point in time that the information comes across, your so-called "reputation" may be at stake. So what!

As an example, let's assume that you are a wildly successful author and public speaker on the subject of genetic engineering. You also happen to be a bit of an introvert and someone who doesn't enjoy small talk. You give a speech, for whatever reason, to a large group of salespeople. Most salespeople are social by nature and appreciate small talk. Because of this, your demeanor at this event may not make the best impression and others may see you as arrogant, egotistical, vain, superior or stand-off-ish.

Some are so focused on what others think of them that they spend an inordinate amount of time feeling slighted when they perceive that they are not being given the value or respect that they deserve. Do you get offended easily and often? Psychologists call these slights 'narcissistic injuries' because they bruise our egos. Do you become angry and resentful when someone neglects to acknowledge you? Think about how you feel when a friend doesn't call you on your birthday or when a colleague questions something that you've put in a work report. If you find that you are frequently offended by words and situations, this stems from a perceived threat to identity, which is of the ego.

Is there really nothing that can be done about this? If your sole aim and purpose is to get people to like you and "manage" your reputation, you are working solely from ego and missing the boat entirely. If, on the other hand, you are following your bliss in life and treating other people as you would want to be treated, then thoughts of reputation should not even enter the picture.   If you are worrying about reputation, you are taking time away from doing the things that really matter.

Reputation is an idle and most false imposition; oft got without merit, and lost without deserving. - *William Shakespeare, Othello*

Ego Says I Am

Sometime I think; and sometime I am. - *Paul Valéry*

In the previous chapters we talked about how ego drives the way we define ourselves through our possessions, our careers and achievements, and by our reputation. All of this is true and, taken to the next level, ego can absolutely dictate how we construct our feelings of self worth and develop the ways that we relate to the outside world. When relying solely on ego, we are given many messages that are contrary to the achievement of that happy and fulfilling life that most of us actually desire.

Ego Says I Am: Lacking

Not necessity, not desire - no, the love of power is the demon of men. Let them have everything - health, food, a place to live, entertainment - they are and remain unhappy and low-spirited: for the demon waits and waits and will be satisfied. - Friedrich Nietzsche

Ego tells us constantly that we are lacking in life by the things that we desire the most. It could be the right relationship, a better job, a nicer home, or a stronger spiritual connection. It doesn't matter. The point is that ego sends us a never-ending string of messages that tells us that what we have right now is never "good enough" and we'd be happy with something else. These are all negative thoughts and, if you know anything about The Law of Attraction, they are entirely counter-productive. I am a firm believer in the notion that what we think upon grows and, by constantly bombarding our lives with thoughts of what's missing, we are simply inviting more of that lack into our existence. In the now famous words of Bob Newhart - "Stop It!".

If we want to love our lives and do exciting things, this is a moment by moment choice, plain and simple. Of course, most people strive to make improvements in their lives either personally or professionally. However, the way to go about it isn't to whine about the way things are now, wish things were different and scheme to get ahead. Negative thinking will not produce positive changes - ever. We'll delve more deeply into some action steps for making some of these shifts in the following chapters.

When you are discontent, you always want more, more, more. Your desire can never be satisfied. But when you practice contentment, you can say to yourself, 'Oh yes - I already have everything that I really need.' - Dalai Lama

Ego Says I Am: Separate From Others

When we separate ourselves from the rest of the world, the world becomes a lonely and difficult place to live in. When we see ourselves as completely separate, we cannot call upon the power and strength that comes from unity, from being part of a greater whole. - Tom Walsh

One of the key beliefs of the ego is that we are separate from each other. When we nurture these feelings of separation, we are also fostering feelings of competition, which is something that was discussed in the last section. When we are identifying ourselves based upon our possessions and our achievements, there is always competition and comparison. This inevitably leads to fear, resentment and a host of other negative emotions that you're not likely to enjoy.

When we allow our ego to tell us that we are separate from everyone else, what we are really doing is making a judgment. By cutting ourselves off from others, we are either saying that we are better or worse than someone else or that we have nothing in common with anyone else and shouldn't bother. All of these notions are faulty and are ego's perfect message designed to keep us isolated. We can be isolated as individuals, as groups or some combination thereof. Our separate ways of thinking over the ages have led to such beliefs as:

- Our race is better than your race
- Our political system is superior to yours
- The final score shows that I am the winner and you are the loser
- Our religion is the only pathway to God
- Men are smarter than women
- and so on

E-Go

Let's face it - most of us would prefer happiness over misery. It's a fact that happiness doesn't come through isolation. A recent 20-year study of more than 4,000 people showed that happiness is influenced not just by your immediate friends and family. The happiness of a friend of a friend of a friend -- someone you've never even met -- can also influence your happiness. It turns out that happiness can spread through social networks, like a virus.

However, if we remain self-absorbed in our own little worlds, with our self-constructed problems, it's hard to see the big picture and life can become a vicious cycle of discomfort and misery. By making just a few connections with others and starting to build some common ground, we begin to see that we aren't separate after all. What's the best way to make these connections? Easy! Compassion and service.

If you want others to be happy, practice compassion; if you want to be happy, practice compassion. - 14th Dalai Lama

Ego Says I Am: Separate From God

It's not what you look at that matters, it's what you see. - Henry David Thoreau

First and foremost, this isn't a Christian or religious book at all. Many people do not believe in a higher power and that's absolutely their right. All I ask when reading these sections is that you only keep an open mind about what is discussed because it is at this point that we begin to talk of free will, duality and God. If you prefer the term Universal Source, I often use that as well. The key point here is, if you think that you are running the show, therein lies the problem.

This is one of my favorite stories about duality and separation from God:

A professor at the university asked his students a question:
- Everything that exists was created by God?
One student answered bravely:
- Yes, created by God.
- God created everything? - asked the professor.
- Yes, Sir, - the student answered.
Professor asked:
- If God created everything, that means that God created evil, because it exists. And according to this principal, the things we do determine who we are, that means - God is evil.
The student got quiet after hearing that answer. Professor was very happy with himself. He boasted to the students, that he proved once again that God is a myth. Another student raised his hand and said:
- Can I ask you a question, professor?
- Of course, - professor answered.
The student got up and asked:
- Professor, does cold exist?
- What kind of question is this? Of course it exists. Didn't you ever get cold?

E-Go

Students laughed at the question of the young man. The young man answered:
- Actually, Sir, cold doesn't exist. According to the laws of physics, what we consider to be cold truthfully is the absence of heat. You can study a person or a thing according to its ability to transfer energy. An absolute zero (-460 degrees according to Fahrenheit) is a complete absence of heat. The whole substance becomes inert and unable to react in that temperature. Cold doesn't exist. We created that word to describe what we feel at the absence of heat.
The student continued:
- Professor, does the darkness exist?
- Of course it exists.
- You are wrong again, Sir. The darkness also doesn't exist. Darkness is actually the absence of light. We can study the light, but not the darkness. We can use the prism of Newton to expand the white light into many colors and study the different lengths of the waves of each color. You can't measure the darkness. A simple ray of light can burst into the world of darkness and light it up. How can you find out how dark some kind of a space is? You measure the quantity of light submitted. Isn't it? Darkness is an understanding which people use to describe something that happens in the absence of light.
Finally, the young man asked the professor:
- Sir, does evil exist?
This time timidly, professor answered:
- Of course, as I have already said. We see it every day. Cruelty among the people, lots of crimes and violence around the world. These examples are nothing other than the manifestations of evil.
The student answered to this:
- Evil doesn't exist, Sir, at least, it doesn't exist for itself. Evil – is just an absence of God. It is similar to darkness and cold, created by people, to describe the absence of God. God didn't create evil. Evil is not faith or love, which exists like light and heat. Evil – is the result of absence of Godly love in a human heart. It's like the cold, which comes when there is no heat, or like the darkness, which comes when there is no light.
The Professor sat down.

First let's talk about duality. This is the idea that we have two essential parts, and both must exist on some level. Before our creation, there was only God, or the Universal Source, and so only Love. After our creation, man was on a physical plane and was given what we call free will. We could make choices and feel a wide range of emotions. Regardless if those choices were about survival or luxuries, they increasingly stemmed from a place of self-centered fear (ego) and took us further and further away from where we originated - our Source.

Ego, in this sense, was born the moment that man turned away from God. *A Course in Miracles* refers to this thought of having been separated from God as "a tiny mad idea". In the biblical realm you can point to the Garden of Eden forbidden fruit story. Otherwise, this can simply mean that at some point we decided to start listening to that little voice in our heads that said "this way is better" rather than follow the path of Universal Love. That ego voice then comes up with all sorts of ideas and schemes to get us what we want, yet never seems to deliver the goods (true happiness) in the end.

So, have we truly separated from God? In reality, this is not possible but we are really just playing with semantics here. What has happened is that we perceive we are separate and behave as such, with all of the guilt and suffering thrown in for good measure. With this separation, you have been operating along the lower energy continuum of ego and all of the false beliefs that reside there. The higher energy, or your true self, is the part of you that is one with God. The reality is that the Universal Source was never separate and never went anywhere. It has been waiting patiently and lovingly for you to wake up from this dream of separation and become one with your true nature.

A sense of separation from God is the only lack you really need correct. - A Course in Miracles

The Picture of a Life Run on Ego

The ego is a fascinating monster.   - Alanis Morissette

Before we get into the various ways, including action steps, that you can take to reduce the ego's dominance in your life, let's take a look at several examples of lives that are run predominantly on ego and the different ways that this can be manifested.   While it is true that everything on earth has a will - every flower, every blade of grass, every animal - the will does not behave the same across all of them.   In fact, most living things conform to an eternal call of being, growing, living and dying. Only humans and domestic animals have defied these laws with their self-willed behavior, where ego becomes a factor.   We're only going to discuss the human condition here, leaving Fido out of it, and three ways in which a life run on ego is manifested.   Each of these three is described as an extreme and, while some people may find that they fit into just one of these extreme categories, a majority will be able to relate a little bit to various elements expressed in each one of them.

Part of me suspects that I'm a loser, and the other part of me thinks I'm God Almighty. - John Lennon

The Winner

If there's anything more important than my ego around, I want it caught and shot now. - Douglas Adams

The Winner is a self-centered person who has to get to the top, or stay there, at all costs. This drive to be the best carries through in all areas of their lives - personal and professional - and it's never-ending. The self-centered winner never takes the time to understand another person's point-of-view or feelings. The self-centered, ego-driven person, is more concerned with their image and their materialistic things than anything else, including events that may affect those close to them. If you are not sure whether this fits you or not, consider these questions:

- Have you spent an entire evening with a friend without once caring about how he or she was feeling? That's not a good sign.

- Have you offended people a number of times, and felt genuinely confused and surprised when you were called out on your actions?

- Have you found yourself going on and on about yourself while a friend is clearly too upset or distracted to listen?

- Do you spend a lot of time rehashing what you said, how many times you made people laugh, or which people in a social situation were clearly attracted to you after you leave a conversation?

Those who are very self-centered may even go as far as lying or manipulating to get their way or make things work out in a way that favors them. A study entitled the "fixed total sacrifice effect" illustrates what it is to be completely self-centered. Subjects who had previously been diagnosed as self-centered were given something that they wanted and that others in the room needed. It was concluded that those who are self-centered use a "two-stage reasoning," in which they determine the amount they want to keep for themselves and then distribute the remaining amount, if any, among those who are actually in need.

A lot of people make the mistake of assuming that the person in this category has a high sense of self-esteem. This may or may not be true. The Winner certainly doesn't have a healthy sense of self-esteem. We discuss what this looks like a bit later. Rather, it is either overly-inflated or a very low sense of self-esteem.

It is quite common for those with a low sense of self-esteem to behave in this manner in an effort to boost the ego. We create grandiose personas out of our insecurities and use these to get attention. Maybe we like to display our expertise in various matters to others to boost our false sense of self. What is worse is that others with these same issues tend to pile onto our bandwagon, and we onto theirs, in order to affirm our false illusions of self. Sometimes we even bully and ridicule others whose views differ from our own in very subtle displays of our insecurities.

The Winner keeps score, wants to be number one and wants to make sure that everyone knows it. These are all extreme statements and most people exhibit some of these traits in some form or another. The importance is to recognize whether or not these ego-driven behaviors are ruling your life so that you can move away from this self-centered behavior. Also, self-centeredness is not the same thing as Narcissism. Self-centered people CAN change while a narcissist generally cannot because the behaviors are hard-wired into their psyche. For the most part, those who want to change can do so and make a beginning with a just a little bit of willingness.

Power over others is weakness disguised as strength. - Eckhart Tolle

The Loser

Negativity is not intelligent. It always of the ego. - *Eckhart Tolle*

Have you ever thought to yourself, or even said out loud:

- "I am just the worst....".
- "I am the ugliest...".
- "I am the stupidest...".
- "I'm so fat..."

Believe it or not, this is ego all the way. When you overly rely on self-deprecation by constantly belittling yourself or diminishing your accomplishments, this is ego shouting for some attention and some reinforcement. The exact same is true when you engage in self-destructive behaviors, such as any sort of sabotaging or self-punishing.

There are exceptions to this, of course, when we refer to certain psychiatric disorders. So, not everyone that exaggerates negative situations or claims emotional devastation is doing so to attract attention. Some have legitimate, and very serious, psychological disturbances that should be dealt with immediately. On the other hand, if you find yourself seeking emotional support and affirmation from others by exaggerating negative characteristics about yourself, consider that this may be an ego-feeding exercise.

Some may wish to argue that this is just low self-esteem. While that may be the case, examine the implications of that. In God's world we are all perfect, equal and divine. When you are making the judgment that you are either less than or better than someone else, you have separated yourself from that world and are living in ego. So, when you make the choice to have your reality be that of "I am the worst...", you are also making the choice to be separate and alone.

Self-pity is egotism undiluted, after all—self-centeredness in its purest form. - *Rick Yancey*

Taite Adams

The Martyr

Evil requires the sanction of the victim. - *Ayn Rand*

Many of us probably think we've known someone, I know I have, with a martyr complex in this lifetime and hopefully we're not that person. First and foremost, let's talk about what a martyr is and isn't. What we are talking about here is emotional manipulation to the extreme. If you look up the term "martyr" online, there will plenty of references to historical and religious figures, such as Christ and the apostles, who died to honor God. This isn't what we're talking about at the moment.

The Martyr that we're discussing in this context is someone who seeks out the feeling of being a victim or of being persecuted for its own sake because it feeds an internal need. A martyr may sometimes seem like someone heroic on the surface because they appear to do so much for others, but the motivations for those actions is what creates the problem. In its most extreme manifestations, this could be a psychological issue. Otherwise, this is a victim complex and it is ego-based, evidenced by a long list of characteristics:

- They expect to be recognized and rewarded for their suffering and sacrifices.

- They have the need to be a victim and complain always and relentlessly.

- They are easily offended when not praised for their sacrifices often enough.

- They expect everyone to be mind-readers and form lasting resentments when unspoken wishes aren't fulfilled.

- They take little initiative in trying to fix any complaint, whether spoken or internalized.

- If any problem is solved according to their solution, they will find something else to suffer about.

- If any problem is solved, it is because they complained about it.

- They complain about problems that do not concern them in the least.

- They do not appreciate any good things being done.

- They lie and twist facts to prove their point.

- They selectively forget, ignore or avoid any facts that may conflict with their point.

- They typically avoid any form of relief, such as therapy, which may end or lessen their suffering.

The whole idea here is that the Martyr's suffering is so extreme that they are convinced that someone else will surely step up and take the blame. The Martyr feels constantly oppressed by powerful forces in this world, claims they are powerless to do anything about it and denies any fault or involvement whatsoever. This is a sideways manifestation of self, plain and simple. Whether built from early negative experiences, misconceptions about life, or a sense of insecurity, it is an extreme example of ego taking hold with a twisted strategy to protect the self.

It is pretty rare that people are able to see clearly that they fit into this category and are then able to do something about it. However, it's not uncommon that we all have a few of these tendencies. Heck, I can read through this list today and check off a few that I still practice occasionally. We are all human. What is key to recognize if you do find yourself exhibiting some of these behaviors is that there is a way out. Being perpetually in control, nurturing fears and holding onto suffering aren't healthy behaviors and it is quite possible to move away from these ego-driven actions.

We are taught you must blame your father, your sisters, your brothers, the school, the teachers - but never blame yourself. It's never your fault. But it's always your fault, because if you wanted to change you're the one who has got to change.   - Katharine Hepburn

Taite Adams

The Opposite of Ego

Judge Not... - Jesus

Nothing is either good or bad, but thinking makes it so. - William Shakespeare

The above quote from Shakespeare is a great one but I'd like to make one little adjustment to it and then we'll dig further:

Nothing is either good or bad, but judging makes it so.

When I pass a judgment about something, I am injecting my own flawed belief system onto it and this takes me away from where I want to be, which is in a state of joy and peace. We relate several popular stories and parables in this book to get some key points across, but here is one of the oldest and most meaningful:

Adam and Eve were thrown out of the Garden of Eden. Wait a minute! That's not right at all. In fact, Adam and Eve stepped out of the Garden (which is Heaven) because they made a choice to bite the forbidden fruit from the tree of knowledge of good and evil (which is ...Judgment). The fruit represents Knowledge itself, which is the opposite of innocence. Did the all-knowing God anticipate what would happen here? I think that question answers itself. While there is good in this world, there is also now evil, which are thoughts of greed, anger, jealousy and such. This is where ego is born and begins to provide justification for these thoughts. Now, with the dreaded deed done (fruit bitten), all these two had to do was to turn around and walk back into the Garden (Heaven). They didn't, of course. Instead, they started blaming. Adam blamed Eve: "She made me do it". Eve blamed that dirty, no-good snake - the ego itself.

The most interesting thing about this is that it was all born of judgment, or choice, as is any notion that we are locked out of Heaven. Consider this: when you are in your own house, you have no need of a key. It's a non-issue. It's the same thing with Heaven. When you are in Heaven, or one with the Universal Source, you aren't searching for a "key" to get in. Yet, when we perceive that we are somehow locked out, we search high and low for that transcendental key that will get us back in. It's really no big Secret. That key is, has always been, and always will be: Love.

The separation was not an act, but a thought. - A Course in Miracles

Taite Adams

Love

The moment you have in your heart this extraordinary thing called love and feel the depth, the delight, the ecstasy of it, you will discover that for you the world is transformed. - Jiddu Krishnamurti

The idea that love is the one and only answer may either come across as very profound to you or pretty trite, as in you've had this bag of goods handed to you before and it's a bunch of baloney. Either way, stick with me. Love really is the answer to all of your problems because love is what brings us back to our Universal Source. I can promise you that the Universal Source wants nothing for you other than for you to be happy, healthy and prosperous in this life. If these are also the things that you want for yourself, I would hope, then what's the issue?

The issue for most of us remains fear. Fear of the unknown is huge and ego gets involved here to the n-th degree. Ego looks at change from a sense of loss and lacking, trying to hold onto what it already has or thinks it has, whether it is miserable or not. Our egoic mind's purpose is to create separation and, when there is an unknown, it will look to events of the past to validate that something will or will not work. Our mind will tell us, "You see, we tried this 'love thing' last year and so-and-so was disrespectful to us. It's worthless."

Here's a novel idea: Treat the unknown as friendly. Consider the idea, it's a fact really, that we live in an intelligent and supportive universe that is designed to support you. Remember that I opened up this section talking about judgments. Well, in reality, life is a never-ending series of judgments and choices and what this is about is learning to re-direct our thinking to the more loving and positive judgments as opposed to the ego-based ones. One of my favorite Albert Einstein quotes is: "I think the most important question facing humanity is, 'Is

~ 51 ~

the universe a friendly place?' This, for most of us, is a moment by moment choice. What is yours going to be right now? If you choose the negative, you have a chance to choose again, and then again. How about now?

If we make the choice to see the universe as friendly, this means that we are a part of a divine order, which is love. Love in the sense that we are talking about here isn't romantic love or even gushy sentiment. This love refers to the thoughts that go through your mind and now you've been handed the ultimate exercise in mind control. What are some of the toughest thoughts to control? The negative ones, of course. In order to embrace the power of love in your life and move away from ego, one of the key elements is to learn how to forgive.

Forgiveness is Key

Forgiveness is not always easy. At times, it feels more painful than the wound we suffered, to forgive the one that inflicted it. And yet, there is no peace without forgiveness. - *Marianne Williamson*

Is there someone with whom you still hold great resentment for some reason or another? The subject of forgiveness is a touchy one for many because it's a concept that has simply been taken off of the table when it comes to some very great hurts in their lives. This is a grave mistake. If you feel that someone doesn't deserve your forgiveness because of a past gross betrayal, you are not alone. Let's take a look at some tried and true ideas about forgiveness, resentment, and even sin.

I am a huge Emmet Fox fan and find that his spiritual teachings have much to say about forgiveness and resentment. In fact, Fox states that the "forgiveness of sins is the central problem of life". He also believes, as do I, that one of the great sins is for us to believe that we live a separate and independent existence, for those that do tend to breed resentment, condemnation, jealousy and remorse. If we were not living this way - in other words, if we were living in the Truth in that all things are One, there would never be anything to forgive in the first place. Since this is a mighty pill for even the most spiritual among us to swallow, there are a few other productive ways to look at forgiveness.

Many of us are just looking for peace in our lives. If you're looking to stay in fear, anger and indignation, this probably isn't the book for you. However, if you are looking for lasting peace and happiness, that is never going to come while you hold onto resentments and refuse to grant forgiveness - to anyone and everyone. It's a fact that when you hold onto feelings of anger and bitterness, the person being hurt the most is you. These negative feelings have an adverse effect on your physical, emotional and even spiritual well-being. By denying forgiveness, you are not only continuing to harm yourself, you are perpetuating a connection to that person, thing or situation that you resent. Consider these wise words from Emmet Fox on the matter:

Setting others free means setting yourself free, because resentment is really a form of attachment. It is a cosmic truth that it takes two to make a prisoner; a prisoner and a jailer. There is no such thing as being a prisoner on one's own account. Moreover, the jailer is as much a prisoner as his charge. When you hold resentment against anyone, you are bound to that person by a mental chain. You are tied by a cosmic tie to the thing that you hate. The one person perhaps in the whole world whom you most dislike is the very one to whom you are attaching yourself by a hook that is stronger than steel. Is this what you wish? Is this the condition in which you desire to go on living? Remember, you belong to the thing with which you are linked in thought, and at some time or other, if that tie endures, the object of your resentment will be drawn again into your life, perhaps to work further havoc. No one can afford such a thing; and so you must cut all such ties by a clear act of forgiveness.

Makes sense, right? It might make perfect sense, and it does, but many people will still respond with "Yeah, but my situation is different and I have a right to be angry". It is incredibly common and one of the toughest barriers to peace. First, let's look at what refusing to forgive others is providing you:

- Ongoing spiritual and emotional turmoil
- Anxiety, stress and hostility
- High blood pressure and other potential health problems
- Symptoms of depression and anxiety disorder
- Greater risk of alcohol and substance abuse

Sure - Who wouldn't want to get rid of that happy list? Remember, forgiveness is all about you and your release from these bonds. It really doesn't have very much to with the other person or situation at

Taite Adams

all. In fact, forgiveness frees us to become the person that we've always wanted to be, and were meant to be, yet couldn't approach because of being held back by resentment and negativity. Many people mistakenly believe that by forgiving, they must forget past hurts and become friends or allies with people who have harmed them. This is not the case at all. We are not obliged to like everyone, only to love and forgive everyone, sometimes from a distance. Often, the person that needs forgiveness the most is ourselves.

When we have a hard time moving forward in life because we are stifled by guilt and shame, self-forgiveness becomes a big issue. Many people can stay trapped for years and not have any idea why they are so bogged down in all of their actions. Holding back self-forgiveness brings forth the same set of symptoms in your life that refusing to give forgiveness to others does. In case you've forgotten what those are in just a few pages, here they are again:

- Ongoing spiritual and emotional turmoil
- Anxiety, stress and hostility
- High blood pressure and other potential health problems
- Symptoms of depression and anxiety disorder
- Greater risk of alcohol and substance abuse

Regardless of whether you need to forgive someone else, some untenable situation or yourself, it's time to take some action and Let It Go! A life lived mired in resentment is one that is lived primarily in the past and this is never one that is filled with joy. You can only think one thought at a time. If you are constantly re-playing tapes from the past, you aren't living in the present and this is where the real magic is happening. Are you feeling un-connected with others? Hint - they are here in the present, not back in the past where you are likely spending an inordinate amount of time. Let's figure out how to move away from that place and forgive, which is the essence of love.

So how do we forgive? Are you willing to forgive? If so, you are nearly there because finding that place of becoming willing to let something go is the greatest part of the work. If you are not willing to forgive, consider the reasons why and take another look at that list of things that holding onto resentments are doing to YOU, not to them. Because, frankly, many times the people that we resent either have no idea about it or could care less. I heard someone say recently that holding onto a resentment is like setting yourself on fire and hoping that the other person dies of smoke inhalation. Insanity, right? In essence, we are allowing them to live "rent free" in our heads and it's time to boot them out.

If you are willing to forgive someone, here is a suggestion: Take a few quiet moments alone. Either meditate or read some spiritual material that is meaningful to you. Then, quietly say, "I fully forgive (state the name of the person or situation). I let go of this now for good. It is finished forever and I have no further resentment about this matter. We both are set free. Thank you God". That's it. Don't repeat this over and over again on the same situation as it is a done deal. If thoughts continue to come up about the person or event, they should have lost some of their power. When they do arise, simply state a short reminder about the situation having been dealt with and forgiven - you have moved on.

If you are not willing to forgive, there are few things that you can do. One, you can continue to live in your misery and indignation for as long as you wish. That is certainly your right. However, if you are looking for release from this and are having a hard time letting go of resentment, there is help still. Consider praying for the willingness to forgive. This does work and there is no wrong way to pray. Another suggestion is to pray for the person against whom you have the resentment. This was suggested to me many years ago and I can attest that this also works very well. Pray for a set period of time, say two weeks, and ask that that person be given everything that you would want for yourself, whether you mean it or not. I generally ask that the person be provided with health, happiness and prosperity and find that, after several days, I begin to mean it and the feelings of resentment fade away.

If you believe in lower and higher energies, as I do, it's no secret that holding onto feelings of anger, hatred and resentment keep you at some of the lowest energy levels. It's a proven fact that, in muscle testing, when you are thinking thoughts of revenge, you are weak, while thoughts of love and forgiveness keep you strong. While physical strength is all well and good, forgiveness offers the forgiver so much more. If you would like a life that is more serene, healthier, more spiritual, and full of healthier relationships, this is definitely for you.

It's one of the greatest gifts you can give yourself, to forgive. Forgive everybody. - Maya Angelou

Thoughts Are Things

...to say a thing 'must be', is the very power that makes it. - Prentice Mulford

I enjoy reading the teachings of the New Thought Movement writers and Prentice Mulford wrote about the power of thought in the late 1800's, long before our contemporaries grabbed onto it and made it popular. Mulford describes our two minds, the mind of the body and the mind of the spirit. He states that the mind of the body (driven by ego) is limited and fights change. In contrast, the mind of the spirit is connect to the Universal Source and knows that anything is possible if you just believe. There is some ground-breaking Law of Attraction language in this 100+ year old book and I highly recommend that anyone interested grab a copy. Essentially, though, Mulford tells us that where we dedicate our attention is essential, including staying in the moment.

I have found in my own experience that thoughts are powerful beyond measure. When we have a thought about something, that is all it is at the outset. Just a thought. As human beings, however, we "claim" these thoughts and generally give them a label based upon our past experience or, in many cases, the experience of our parents or other early influences. Once we claim enough of these thoughts, they eventually form our beliefs. These beliefs then become facts and those facts turn into our truth. What is the truth for me based upon a single thought may not be, and probably isn't, the same thing for you, and vice versa.

A Course in Miracles has a very profound thing to say about thoughts, which I happen to agree with. "Only my thoughts can hurt me". Ponder that one for a moment. Again, we can only think one thought at a time and if I am choosing to think thoughts that I don't enjoy, whose fault is that? Any suffering on my part, at any time, is unnecessary suffering. I always have the choice in what thoughts I am thinking and this has everything to do with love, forgiveness and moving away from ego through the essentials of being present, kindness, and appreciation.

All that we are is the result of what we have thought. The mind is everything. What we think we become. - Buddah

Be Present

You must live in the present, launch yourself on every wave, find your eternity in each moment. - *Henry David Thoreau*

Do you tend to spend time replaying old conversations or events in your head, wishing things had turned out differently or arranging events with different outcomes so that maybe you said something more witty or profound at a particular moment in time? I know I've wasted plenty of time doing this. Do you spend a lot of time worrying about some future event, scheming ways to make things turn out the way you desperately desire? Guilty here too.

When we do either of these things, we are saying that the present isn't good enough and this is looking at life through a sense of loss instead of abundance. Remember, ego always tells us that something is missing when, in reality, this isn't so at all. So, if I am suffering pain because of past events or am anxious about the future, there is no room for me to enjoy the splendor of the present. And, again, this is where all of the magic is happening.

Someone once told me that when we are living in the moment, everything is perfect. That seemed a bit simplistic to me until I was given a pretty profound exercise to consider. I was reminded how many seconds are in a minute, and then a day and so forth. The number of seconds in a year comes out to 31,536,000. Now, if I were to take that number and multiply it by my current age (44 and then some), I would find out that I have been on this earth for approximately 1.4 Billion seconds. And for each and every 1.4 Billion of those seconds, I have been just fine. What sort of arrogance would it be for me to say, "well, sure I've been fine for the last 1.4 billion seconds, but I'm pretty sure that the next one is going to be a disaster".

Our lack of faith in the loving, intelligent and friendly universe is sometimes astounding.

So, how do we stay present? This is really another book in itself and "living in the Now" takes practice but the results are certainly worth every grain of effort. Understanding how wasteful it is that life is simply passing us by as we spend our lives in anyplace but the present moment is a great start. Changing the way we look at the past through forgiveness, of ourselves and others, can work wonders as well. This allows us to simply let go of old hurts and move on to more enjoyable and productive matters - like what's happening right now. Other things you can do to practice staying present include practicing meditation, being mindful of your surroundings, and embracing perfection all around you.

The ability to be in the present moment is a major component of mental wellness. - Abraham Maslow

Taite Adams

Meditation

The language of God is silence. Everything else is a poor translation. - *Rumi*

The first time someone suggested meditation to me, about fifteen years ago, I thought that it was the most hocus-pocus exercise and a colossal waste of my time. I was also wound up tighter than a top and my life was in such a shambles that I had run out of options. They say that pain is a great motivator. While I can't say that meditation did wonders for me right out of the gate, over the years it has opened some doors to a lasting peace that I never thought I would find. Meditation, for me, is usually coupled with some sort of prayer ritual but everyone's experience with this is different.

What meditation really does is bring a person to the present by having you concentrate on your breath. When concentrating on the breath, it is less likely that the mind will wander and, if it does, it is easier to bring it back to the simple act of breathing in and out. Meditation can be done alone, in groups, with guided meditation tapes, YouTube videos, and even smartphone apps. The best way to get the most out of meditation? Practice!

E-Go

Be Mindful

Walk as if you are kissing the Earth with your feet. - Thích Nh□ t H□ nh

We were given the gift of five senses (touch, taste, sight, smell and sound) and these wonderful gifts can help us to stay in the present moment through the practice of mindfulness. Nature is a wonderful place to practice using these gifts but you can try this anywhere - at your office desk, your dinner table, driving in the car, or sitting on the couch. Take a few deep breaths and consider all of the information that your senses are providing to you at that moment in time. Ask yourself these questions:

- What is the texture of the floor like beneath your feet?
- Is there a breeze against your skin?
- If your hands are on your lap, what does the fabric of your clothing feel like?
- Can you smell anything right now?
- If you're at the office, can you smell coffee from the lunchroom or a co-worker's desk?
- If you're at home or outside, try to pinpoint a few scents that you can recognize.
- Can you tune into the bubbles fizzing in your drink?
- The ticking of a clock in another room?
- Do you hear traffic? Raindrops? Birds?
- Let your eyes rest on an item near you, and really look at it, even if it's something that's in your peripheral vision every day.
- Is it a plant that you can look at and analyze in detail?

Immerse yourself in physical sensations and really be aware of what everything feels like. Take a moment to really listen to the world around you. Most of us acclimatize to our living conditions so much that we tune out most of what we hear over the course of the day, so keep your eyes closed and listen - don't just hear. When you take a bite or sip of something, give the food your entire attention: notice the textures, the different flavors. Pay attention to the movement your tongue and throat make as you eat, and see if you can focus on the item you've swallowed as it makes its way down to your stomach. Use your God-given senses as tools to help you practice mindfulness and experience the magic of the present moment.

Embrace Perfection

Every particular in nature, a leaf, a drop, a crystal, a moment of time is related to the whole, and partakes of the perfection of the whole. - Ralph Waldo Emerson

One of the most amazing things about the present is that it's always perfect. Nothing needs improving if we accept that things happen just as they are supposed to happen, when they are supposed to happen. There may at times be things happening in the present moment that we choose to label as disagreeable but I've come to learn that these things are not random at all. In fact, all of life's happenings and all of our encounters are perfection itself. We can certainly justify that they are "random" until we are blue in the face but this is not the case. The truth of the matter is that, at the perfect moment, our perfect lesson is always in front of us. There is always an opportunity for salvation in that moment and we are given a choice in every single moment. If we choose in the negative, there is nothing wrong with that. Another opportunity will present itself soon enough.

It is the nature of the human condition, and the essence of ego domination itself, to believe that we are somehow flawed and in need of improvement. To truly believe that life is just a series of accidents, missed opportunities and unforgivable sins is a grave disservice to your very soul. The truth is that each and every moment is perfect, containing a gift for each person's individual experience. While these experiences may not always feel like "gifts", they each have a special purpose, designed to give you what you need in order for you to evolve into a higher level of consciousness. You are a divine manifestation of the process of creation, which is perfection itself. Embrace this!

Always say 'yes' to the present moment... Surrender to what is. Say 'yes' to life - and see how life starts suddenly to start working for you rather than against you. - Eckhart Tolle

Be Kind

Three things in human life are important: the first is to be kind; the second is to be kind; and the third is to be kind. - Henry James

Our ego tends to give us some the worst, counter-productive, information and advice when it comes to dealing with others and getting what we want. Let's take kindness as an example. Ego tells us that, in order to succeed in life, you need to think only of yourself and ignore the needs of others. It may also whisper to us that kindness is a sign of weakness. These messages from the ego about kindness are the polar opposite of the truth. Not only that, withholding kindness is just not nice.

The truth about kindness is that it comes right from a place of love and this is a fundamental attribute of the Universal Source. Remember the discussion about how what we think upon grows? This certainly holds true with kindness. If I am holding unkind thoughts about what is wrong with the world and the people around me, being offended at every turn, I am sure to get more of those things that I dislike placed in my path. Conversely, if I see things and act in a more kindly manner, the universe responds accordingly.

So, what does kindness mean anyway? This can be pretty ambiguous to some. It doesn't have to be complicated at all. Being kind can be as simple as exercising good manners where you had none before. Say please, thank you and smile at people when you do so. Kindness doesn't have to take extra hours out of your day or cost you a dime. What matters more than anything else is the intent behind your words and actions, being aware of the people around you, and taking notice of their needs and feelings. The following is a story about an act of kindness that I've read many times but it never seems to get old and always brings a few tears to my eyes:

Many years ago I worked as a taxi cab driver.
One time I had to pick up a passenger in the middle of the night. When I arrived at the address, the building was dark, except a light in a ground floor window. Many drivers would wait just honk, wait for a couple of minutes and drive away in such circumstances. But I thought of passengers that might need my assistance. Therefore I always went to the door and knocked. So I did the same this time too. I heard a weak voice of an elderly woman: "Just a minute". The door opened and I saw a small lady in her 80's, wearing a dress and a pillbox hat. She had a small suitcase in her hands.
So I took the lady's suitcase and helped her to walk to the cab. "Thank you for your kindness" – she said. "It's nothing," – I said. "I just try to treat my passengers the way I would want my mother treated". "You are a very decent person".
When we got into the cab, she told the address and asked: "Could you drive through downtown?". I told her, that it was not the shortest way. "I know, but there is no rush, as I am on my way to a hospice. I have no family left". I noticed tears in her eyes.
I quietly switched of the meter and asked, what route would she like me to take. While we drove through the city, the old lady showed me the places, that were important to her. The building, where she worked as an elevator operator. The house, where she and her husband lived just after their marriage. The warehouse, where there was a ballroom many years ago, so she went dancing there, when she was a young girl.
After two hours of driving she silently said: "I'm tired, let's go now".
As soon as we arrived at the address she gave me, two orderlies came out to the cab. They seemed to be waiting for her. I took the lady's suitcase, while she was seated in a wheelchair. "Tell me, how much do I owe you?" she asked. I said, that she owes me nothing. "But you have to make a living". "There are other passengers", - I replied and gave her a hug. She held onto me tightly. "Thank you for giving me those moments of joy" , – she said.

Taite Adams

When I was walking to the cab, I heard a door shut. I thought to myself that it sounded like closing of person's life.
That day I did not pick up any more passengers, I just drove without any purpose, lost in thoughts about the old lady. What if she had gotten an angry or indifferent driver, who was impatient to end his shift? I seems to me that this drive was the most important thing I've done in my life.
We always look for a great moments, but sometimes great moments catch us unaware, beautifully wrapped in what might be considered as nothing particular.

Of course, the Golden Rule eluded to in this story is a great thing to remember and take to heart, yet kindness is not always a reciprocal gesture. I'm sure we've all heard of the concept of "paying it forward", wherein someone does something nice for you, asking only that you pass on the kindness at some point. What isn't discussed enough are the amazing feelings of goodwill and gratitude that are passed along down that line.

My family walks a few blocks down to the local bowling alley each Saturday evening to shoot a few games of pool. A few weeks ago, there was a table set up inside the door for a bake sale benefitting some local charity or school. We eyed the goodies as we played our games but hadn't committed to purchase anything yet. Then, out of the blue, a gentleman we had never seen before walked up and handed us a whole cake that he had purchased for us. My wife was thrilled and started looking around for someone to that she could "buy something for". There just happened to be a family bowling with several school-aged children in tow. She quickly purchased a whole chocolate cake and took it over. The kids were ecstatic and, after she explained to the mother that someone had given something to us, a smile that hadn't been there before spread across the mother's face as she started to scope out the crowd for someone that she could pass along the kindness to. We walked out of the bowling alley that night feeling closer to each other and feeling a new connection to those about us. One of the most important realizations is that these aren't random occurrences. There are opportunities for these connections and for kindness to others in every moment.

My religion is very simple. My religion is kindness. - Dalai Lama XIV

Appreciation

Gratitude unlocks the fullness of life. It turns what we have into enough, and more. It turns denial into acceptance, chaos to order, confusion to clarity. It can turn a meal into a feast, a house into a home, a stranger into a friend. - Melody Beattie

As we are able to achieve more and more ego distancing through the tools presented so far, thus comes a higher level of what we refer to as emotional intelligence. With this, self becomes less of a concern, priorities become more clear and we begin to hold a greater degree of appreciation for all that life has put in our path. We call this last one gratitude. Finding and expressing gratitude are crucial elements in moving away from ego and re-connecting with our Universal Source.

Robert Emmons, whom some consider one of the world's leading scientific experts on gratitude, says that there are two key components to gratitude. "First," he writes, "it's an affirmation of goodness. We affirm that there are good things in the world, gifts and benefits we've received." In the second part of gratitude, he explains, "we recognize that the sources of this goodness are outside of ourselves. ... We acknowledge that other people—or even higher powers, if you're of a spiritual mindset—gave us many gifts, big and small, to help us achieve the goodness in our lives." Emmons and other researchers see the social dimension as being especially important to gratitude. "I see it as a relationship-strengthening emotion," writes Emmons, "because it requires us to see how we've been supported and affirmed by other people."

Gratitude is a popular subject these past few years. The reason, I believe, is because it is so powerful. Who hasn't heard of the famous book by Norman Vincent Peale called "The Power of Positive Thinking"? We're not going to dissect that book just now but, suffice it to say that living in a state of Gratitude and appreciation is the most powerful method of positive thinking known to man. The benefits of gratitude are nearly endless and absolutely astounding. Here are just a few:

- Gratitude makes us happier by boosting feelings of optimism, joy, and enthusiasm
- Gratitude reduces anxiety and depression
- Studies by Robert Emmons and Michael McCollough suggest that gratitude strengthens the immune system, lowers blood pressure, reduces symptoms of illness, and encourages us to take better care of our overall health
- Gratitude results in a better night's sleep
- Gratitude has been found to help people suffering from PTSD
- Gratitude strengthens relationships, promotes forgiveness, and fosters increased compassion
- Gratitude produces positive emotions and greater life satisfaction in kids

Now that we've outlined the benefits of finding and expressing gratitude, it may still be a struggle for some to cultivate it. That's fine. You are not alone. The world isn't full of naturally grateful people and some of us need some help and perspective when searching for the gratitude in life and in every situation. Here is a great story on gratitude and perspective:

There was a boy, whose family was very wealthy. One day his father took him on a trip to the country, where he aimed to show his son, how poor people live. So they arrived to a farm of a very poor family, as he considered. They spent several days there. On their return, the father asked his son, if he liked the trip.
"Oh, it was great, dad" – the boy replied. "Did you notice, how poor people live?".
"Yeah, I did" – said the boy. The father asked his son to tell in more detail about his impressions from their trip".

"Well, we have only one dog, and they have four of them. In our garden there is a pool, while they have a river, that has no end. We've got expensive lanterns, but they have stars above their heads at night. We have the patio, and they have the whole horizon. We have only a small piece of land, while they have the endless fields. We buy food, but they grow it. We have a high fence for protection of our property, and they don't need it, as their friends protect them."
The father was stunned, he could not say a word.
Then the boy added: "Thank you, dad, for letting me see how poor we are."
This story shows that true wealth as well as happiness are not measured by material things. Love, friendship and freedom are far more valuable.

Gratitude is one of the best tools to remind us of what is really important in life and to connect us to other people through expressing appreciation. If you are still unsure about how to get started, here are a few tips:

- Daily gratitude session - Take some time out each day to ponder the things that you're grateful for. This can be as simple as taking 1-2 minutes in the morning and saying a silent "Thank You" to the universe that all of your basic needs have been met. This is a great start.

- Say Thank You - When someone does something nice for you, however small it may be, say Thank You (out loud) and try to mean it. If you don't mean it at first, keep doing it. You'll get there.

- The Bad Stuff is the Good Stuff - I read a book by this name once and it made profound sense. Who are we to judge what's good and bad? Regardless, we do it anyway and this is the source of our eternal happiness or discontent. Try instead to turn the tables on something that you have labeled as "bad" and see where you can find the good in every situation. If you're boss is being particularly unruly today, remember to give thanks for the fact that you have a job at all. If your children aren't listening to you, again, take another look at those faces and thank God that they are healthy enough to be unruly. There is good to be found in just about every situation. If you can't find it at the moment, that's ok. Ask for help.

- Pray for Gratitude - For anyone who really struggles with this, or just anyone, prayers for help with gratitude can be a great help. There are plenty of them out there so find one that works for you and give it a try. Here's a good one:

I am grateful for my family and friends,
a job to earn my keep, and the health to do it,
and opportunities and the lessons I've learned.
Let me never lose sight of the simple blessings
that form the fabric and foundation of my life,
I am blessed, yesterday, today and tomorrow.

When we express gratitude to others, there is the added benefit of putting kindness into the mix. Mark Twain said, "I can live two months on a good compliment". It's great to give compliments and make others feel good but this is only part of it. As we talked about earlier, expressing gratitude makes the expresser feel good as well and motivates them to do even more. This also creates a bond between the two people that is strengthened with each compliment given.

Feeling gratitude and not expressing it is like wrapping a present and not giving it.
- William Arthur Ward

This ends Section I of the book on the essentials of the ego, although there is much more information along those lines to come. Part II is a series of chapters that deals with ego distancing through mindfulness, emotional intelligence and the language of love in the different areas of our lives - relationships, work and health. In each area, we will take a look at how ego creates barriers in these parts of our lives, what these areas look like when we are able to distance from ego, action steps for ego distancing in these areas and overcoming potential roadblocks.

Section II - Ego Distancing Through Mindfulness, Emotional Intelligence and the Language of Love

We must go beyond the constant clamor of ego, beyond the tools of logic and reason, to the still, calm place within us: the realm of the soul. - *Deepak Chopra*

Ego Distancing in Relationships

How Ego Creates Barriers in Relationships

In the hands of the ego, marriage is a prison. It is exclusive. It is a place where people are constantly reminded of their failures and limited by the energies of another person. It is rife with judgment and blame. - *Marianne Williamson*

It's probably a no-brainer to state that ego causes problems and creates barriers in relationships. If you think about it, there is a whole industry that has sprung up around relationship conflicts. Think Jerry Springer, Dr. Phil and other reality TV shows. If we look at things from those extremes, it's easy to see the ego in play and how selfishness rules people's decisions and tears families apart. Yet, in everyday, normal relationships (those not on MTV), it can oftentimes be more difficult to differentiate the source of the barriers between two people. It all comes down to one word, though: Judgment.

Judgment is the source of most failed relationships, whether we see this and label it as such or not. And where does judgment come from? Why, it's ego-based of course. With Spirit, there is no judgment. Consider a strong personal relationship that you have - it can be a love relationship or one with a very close friend. When you first meet this person, there are probably some very strong feelings and you may be so enchanted that something within you moves. Some aspect of your soul responds and, with time, you begin to feel more and more comfortable with them. Small things are forgiven out of hand, even things that in the past would have really irritated you.

Life is magical and you feel that you have found someone with whom you will have a lasting connection. Then one day, without realizing it, a judgment comes into your mind. It may just be a passing thought of "that's not how I would have done that" or "I never noticed that before". This unspoken judgment may start to build in your mind and can eventually lead to doubt, which leads to more judgment, which builds on itself over time. Both parties may be going through this process and, at some point, separation starts to occur. What's generally happening is that you are more present in the beginnings of these relationships and your subconscious, where ego pops up, is suppressed to a large extent.

At the beginning of this joyous union, you were able to unconsciously silence that little voice of judgment because it was overwhelmed by the yearning for the connection. This little voice is the ego constantly trying to interject judgments into the mix based upon your self-identification and beliefs . However, as the daily grind of life starts to intercede, we are not as conscious as we once were and this is where the subconscious ego sees its opening and pounces. What will ultimately happen is that you will find a way to once again silence that voice by again finding that place where your two souls connected in the beginning, or you will allow your ego to drag you away and begin looking elsewhere for another person to fit a need that you now see as being unmet.

The above scenario describes in pretty abstract terms just how ego distancing creates barriers in relationships. If you had a difficult time relating to those terms, that's ok. Take a moment and think about your motives for being in a relationship at all. Are you thinking about what you can bring to the equation or about what you can get from that person? If you are attempting to "get" something from the other person to fill a need, this is coming from ego. The sorts of needs that we try to fill with relationships include:

- Self-esteem
- Safety/Security
- Power and control
- Physical gratification
- Distraction

Just because someone else is receptive to our wants on this level, doesn't make it ok or healthy. It simply means that their egos are responding to the call of ours and we are fulfilling some need that they also have. The "love" given in these situations has conditions attached and that means that there are rules, whether spoken or not. Any giving between parties is based on the expectation that something will be given in return. At extremes, control and manipulation enter the picture. The greatest extreme is when what we called "love" turns into hate. In these extreme examples, no doubt ego has played a major role as resentments kick in over unmet expectations. Never fun, and sometimes dangerous, these types of relationships are based on lack, not mutual trust and respect as is one with healthy ego distancing.

A Relationship With Healthy Ego Distancing

The meeting of two personalities is like the contact of two chemical substances: if there is any reaction, both are transformed. - C.G. Jung

Imagine a relationship based only on love. There is no resistance, no arguing, no sarcasm, disrespect, blame, competition, distrust, or frustration. Sounds like something out of a sappy Hollywood movie, doesn't it? Believe it or not, while there are no perfect relationships in this world, it is possible to get close to these ideals through both partners distancing from the ego and working together towards such things as: acceptance, forgiveness, trust, understanding, compassion and gratitude.

Healthy relationships can't ever take ego completely out of the equation. This simply isn't possible. The idea is that the parties are connected at the Source, instead of at the lower-level ego. They are bound on a soul level and here there is only love. There are no agendas - no craving to fill a void or to be dominant over the other party. We still nurture ourselves and our own souls so that we are able to give freely to someone else in a relationship, whether it be romantic, friendship or otherwise. While this may sound like a lofty achievement for some, there are solid action steps that can help you arrive at this place of being open to soul-based relationships.

E-Go

Realizing Ego Distancing in Relationships

In this section, you'll find five things to practice in order to make your relationships speak the language of love, and not that of the ego.

Let Go of the Need to be Right

Forgiveness is a lovely idea until you have someone to forgive. -C.S. Lewis

When ego is running the show, you will have an overwhelming desire to prove other people wrong, especially those closest to you. Ego loves a good fight and I used to hold onto arguments and grudges for years, determined to eventually have the last word. At some point I realized that I looked petty and foolish - and the only person that was being harmed by my behavior was - Me! Have you ever heard the saying, "Would you rather be right or happy?" This was profound stuff to me at one point in time! Not anymore - now it's a common theme in my life.

By letting go of your need to be right, you also let go of feelings of anger, resentment, and bitterness that aren't conducive to a soul-based relationship. They're also not conducive to the health and wellness of your own soul and connection with the Source. Do we have to be push-overs then and concede everything? No, not really but I have become pretty astute at picking my battles and it's a pretty rare one that I decide to engage in. I choose to be happy and loving with the people in my life and this seems to unfold better for all involved. If there's a point that you simply can't concede due to some strong principle, someone once suggested that I just look at the person and say, "Perhaps you're right" and leave it at that. I haven't conceded a thing yet it seems to diffuse the situation every time.

In the first section of the book, we talked about forgiveness. This is a key factor in any successful relationship as there will always be conflicts, perceived slights, and differences of opinion. Productive, loving relationships can't exist when one or both parties are holding onto negative feelings, whether from something minor or otherwise. Recognize that everyone is human and remember that, by holding onto feelings of resentment, you are hurting yourself most of all. We can't change other people and the sooner you stop trying by withholding forgiveness, the happier and more content you will be. Forgiveness in relationships doesn't mean that you like everything that the other person does - it means that you accept and love them for who they are.

People who learn to forgive have more successful relationships. Successful couples are able to figure out how to forgive each other for being themselves, and they do this because they know that it is nearly impossible to change other people. Since we are human beings, by definition we are imperfect. - Dr. Fred Luskin

Let Go of Your Need to Be Superior

Monkeys are superior to men in this: when a monkey looks into a mirror, he sees a monkey. - Malcolm de Chazal

Despite growing up an only child, I grew up being very competitive. Perhaps it was being raised in a military family or my delusions of trying to impress the neighborhood kids each time we'd move to a new place. Regardless, living and acting as if I was better than everyone else didn't lend to healthy friendships and relationships. Ego wants us to constantly compare and operate from a state of lack. A need to be superior requires that you continually judge your partner and that isn't going to get you very far, unless you are hoping to get back feelings of anger, resentment and hostility.

Instead, realize that the only person that you need to be better than is the person that you used to be. Life is a constant state of growth and improvements. We grow, uncover, discover and discard old ideas as we move through time and this makes us superior beings from the ones that we were in the past. Otherwise, know in your heart that no one is better or worse than anyone else and that we are all waking up to our oneness with Spirit and each other at different rates. Each person has his own journey yet we are all in Heaven at any given moment. To think and pretend otherwise is pure ego.

Be Present

When you love someone, the best thing you can offer is your presence. How can you love if you are not there? - Thich Nhat Hanh

Remember just a few pages back when we talked about how ego creates barriers in relationships? Dr. Bruce Lipton has a great book out called *The Honeymoon Effect* that discusses this and some of those same concepts about our conscious self and how we revert to the subconscious after a certain period of time, where the ego rules. In other words, we stop being completely present for each other and old ideas creep in.

There are two ways to fix this. One is to re-program the ingrained beliefs and ideas in our sub-conscious, which is entirely possible and which we'll discuss more towards the end of the book. The other is to work on being more present with each other, or more mindful, as there is only love in the present moment. When we are not fully present in our relationships, we emit negative energy that our partner can detect. Mindfulness and being present means we are offering our partner our highest self.

In Buddhism, God is mindfulness and concentration. Every single thing that takes place is exposed to the light of mindfulness and concentration, and that energy of mindfulness and concentration is the essence of the Buddha. Mindfulness and concentration always brings insight, and insight is the factor that liberates us from suffering, because we are able to see the true nature of reality.

If the sound of your partner's voice has become background noise in your life or if, when they are speaking to you, you know that you're just not fully in the room with them, here are some suggestions on how to be present in your relationship:

- When your partner is speaking to you, stop whatever else you are doing and give them your undivided attention.

- If you find yourself distracted or your mind begins wandering as your partner is talking to you, be sure to look them directly in the eyes and remind yourself of the love that you feel for them.

- If you are not fully present because something else is bothering you, such as work or your football pool, be honest about what is going on. When we are honest with our partners instead of pretending that everything is status quo, this fosters love and respect.

- View your partner as someone who deserves the best that you have to give. In other words, listen to them as you would want to be listened to.

Remember that relationships are about relating and staying present is a major part of that. If you are still having difficulty staying present, go back to the chapter on that Section that gives other suggestions for being present, mindful, and even practicing meditation. These things all help you to stay in the present moment, where love resides, but also to distance yourself from ego in your relationships.

Forever is composed of Nows. - Emily Dickinson

Taite Adams

Be Kind

I want to be in a relationship where you telling me you love me is just a ceremonious validation of what you already show me. - Steve Maraboli

How many times have you found yourself in a relationship where the two parties end up struggling just to be nice to each other. Little things like laundry piles, empty toilet paper rolls, and a capless tube of toothpaste have turned into pretty big things and you start to nitpick. There's no longer any such thing as "picking your battles" because everything has turned into one.

If you've ever been to couples therapy or read those self-help books on relationships, a lot of the advice turns to things like "active listening" and validating each other. That's great as far as it goes and helpful if you can both keep up the practice long-term. However, the truth of the matter is that most happy couples aren't doing any of this because they've discovered one of the key secrets to a happy relationship. You have to be nice to each other!

When there is so much to be irritated about, it seems tough to do this sometimes, right? More often than not, the "reason" that couples indicate for the failure of their marriage, on official forms anyway, is "irreconcilable differences". In any great relationship, these are a given! I will always want my partner to put the cap back on the toothpaste and she will always leave it off. There are no two people who are exactly alike in every respect so to try to resolve some of these miniscule differences that are not going to be changed no matter how much you whine, pout or try to lovingly discuss them is futile. These are irresolvable differences and that no longer has to be a negative thing. In fact, it's perfection itself!

What we do instead is identify the big issues that need to be discussed and resolved - and we live with the rest of it. Let go of the need to be right, to be offended, to control a situation, or to change it. It's not going to happen. Instead, focus on the things that you love about your partner and be nice. When you do nice things, they don't need to be big things but they do need to be frequent enough to be noticed and to make a difference. How you practice kindness in any relationship is going to vary. However, if you are having difficulty coming up with any ideas at all on how to be kind to your partner, here are a few to get you started:

- Say something encouraging and complimentary.
- Bust out your manners - Say "Please" and "Thank You", omit the vulgar language, and be courteous in your actions
- Do an act of kindness (such as cleaning the bathroom) and then don't mention it.
- Send a kind note, email or text message.
- Really listen to your partner when they speak to you.
- Smiles, hugs and a simple touch go a long way.
- Ask them: "What can I do for you?", "How are you doing?"

Most people who read books like this are looking to make a change and probably seeking some sort of transformation. There's nothing wrong with that and learning how to distance from ego will surely make monumental changes in your life. However, some the biggest transformations in the lives of individuals and in relationships are based upon those "a-ha moments" that are attributed to somewhat simple ideas. This is one of those. I love this next quote from Aldous Huxley, author of *Brave New World*.

Taite Adams

People often ask me what is the most effective technique for transforming their life. It is a little embarrassing that after years and years of research and experimentation, I have to say that the best answer is—just be a little kinder. - Aldous Huxley

Gratitude

If the only prayer you said in your whole life was, 'thank you,' that would suffice. –
Meister Eckhart

One of the suggestions in the bullet points on "being kind" in the previous chapter was to bust out your manners. This referred partially to expressing thanks to your partner in as many different ways as you can fathom. Gratitude is so important, not only to relationships, but to our entire outlook upon life and the direction that the universe takes us. Have you ever heard the expression, "If you're not happy with what you have, what makes you think you'd be happy with more?" Substitute the word "grateful" for "happy" in that question and it should give you something to ponder, despite the fact that it's not grammatically correct. When ego distancing in relationships, gratitude is a must and it has nothing to do with who deserves our thanks and who doesn't. We need to shell out gratitude like beads at a Mardi Gras parade. This is essential.

Do you ever hold back thanks and gratitude because you feel like people, your partner in particular, are just doing what they're supposed to be doing? If so, you are not alone. Arlie Hochschild has a wonderful theory called "the economy of gratitude" wherein he explains just this sort of thing. Hochschild states that, in relationships, partners offer each other "gifts" which are beyond what is expected or defined as "yours". Therefore, if your "part" is to take care of the trash, the yard and the dishes, your partner is not likely to express gratitude when you do these things and may, in fact, become resentful when you don't do them. Gratitude can go a long way towards changing this dynamic.

By expressing thanks and actually viewing your partner's household labor as a gift, partners tend to feel more appreciated and experience less feelings of resentment. Conversely, when a partner is thanked for anything that they do, regardless of the complexity, it generally gives them a newfound appreciation for those tasks and for the work that the other partner is performing as well. Take time each day to find things about your partner that you are grateful for. Express those beautiful gifts and you'll be sure to get more of them. Positive words and feelings beget positive words, emotions and actions, particularly when it comes to close relationships.

Become an appreciator of everything in your life, not just the household tasks that are being accomplished by your partner. When you say "Thank you God" for everything, you are recognizing and expressing the beauty of the Creator. This becomes internalized for you and it's a fact that you can only give something away that you possess. By being in a state of gratitude in your relationship, you are transported to a higher energy vibration - and that is the language of love.

Lord, grant that I might not so much seek to be loved as to love. - Francis of Assisi

Potential Roadblocks and Solutions

Friendship with one's self is all important, because without it one cannot be friends with anyone else in the world. - *Eleanor Roosevelt*

In the last section, you were given five action steps to help with ego distancing in relationships. Of course, not all relationships can be saved and we're not talking about relationships in which there is abuse or where only one party is present and willing to put in the effort. Sometimes the healthiest thing that we can do is to walk away. We need to take care of ourselves first and that is what this last section is about.

Emotional intelligence is partially about becoming self-aware. If you are having difficulty with your relationship or in finding the relationship that you really desire, you have to take a good look at how you feel about yourself before taking another step. Remember, our actions represent our thoughts and, if you don't think much of yourself, your actions with regards to your partner are going to reflect that. You need to understand, respect, and love yourself first.

No one owes you anything. It is a misconception to think that anyone owes you something, even if you have made sacrifices on their behalf. All actions taken are your choice. Remember the martyr complex talks about being a victim and sacrifice for a reaction or reward does not necessarily make you a good person. When it comes to ego distancing, we've already covered most of the ways to get past this but it can't be repeated often enough. You have to create your joy first, and change your thinking about what you deserve.

As one with the Creator, we are all infinite love and joy and it simply takes realizing this truth to make a start. Do things that make you happy and increase your joy. If you're not sure what those are, keep trying new things. That's half the fun! When you don't feel good about yourself, your energy is low and this radiates out to the world. Look for the positive things in you and focus on those things. As you learn to love and respect yourself, you will also learn to love others and will naturally attract people into your life who will fall in love with you and you will get a cosmic snowball effect of love and joy.

Ego Distancing in Work

How Ego Creates Barriers in Work and Financial Health

If you do not conquer self, you will be conquered by self. - *Napoleon Hill*

Very few people who are driven by ego in their careers are truly happy in their work. While there may be fleeting happiness for a time based on material success and power grabs, this won't last long-term and there is always that internal longing for "more", which is ego telling you that things are never perfect just as they are. Your career choice itself may be highly influenced by ego or the key factor may simply be in how you approach doing your job. When ego takes hold in these areas of our lives, the central focus becomes on such things as:

- Power and titles
- Money and profit
- Personal recognition
- Competition

So many people exist in this state for most of their lives and don't even realize it. In fact, even Deepak Chopra tells a story of how he nearly ruined his medical career by being overcome by ego. He was doing an endocrinology research fellowship in Boston and was put on the spot during a staff meeting by a supervisor. Chopra answered snidely, walked out of the meeting and away from the program altogether. What followed was several years of struggle before he found his way again and what he calls his Dharma, or destiny. Ego doesn't want us to find that and, in fact, is the biggest obstacle to us attaining our true path and becoming who we were meant to be.

A Career With Healthy Ego Distancing

How far you go in life depends on your being tender with the young, compassionate with the aged, sympathetic with the striving and tolerant of the weak and strong. Because someday in your life you will have been all of these. - George Washington Carver

What does a career look like with healthy ego distancing? Well, the career and life path itself will look different for everyone, as it should. Otherwise, expect to find someone who is comfortable where they are at any given moment and who experiences absolute joy as they are pursuing their occupation. That's not to say that there won't be obstacles to overcome along the way. However, as you pursue your life's work, goals are more spirit-driven and you are no longer looking outside for fulfillment.

There are many examples of people who have had successful careers, while at the same time been able to distance from ego and exercise emotional intelligence. Warren Buffet and Tony Hsieh are just a few. One of my favorites, however, is the story of Fred Rogers. An amazing and humble man, Fred Rogers decided to go into children's television in the 1950's because he saw a need for quality, positive programming. He was tolerant to a fault, showed a never-ending interest in other people and had a hyper-dedication to his work. This doesn't mean that he was a push-over. Far from it!

Mr. Rogers stood up before Congress in 1969, when he was still virtually unknown, and spoke out against budget cuts to public television. So impressed with his passion and charm, a budget that was set at $9 million quickly jumped to $22 million. I could go on and on here. In 1997, Fred Rogers was given a Lifetime Achievement Award at the Daytime Emmys. As he always did in public speeches, when he accepted the award he asked the audience to take 10 seconds of silence "to think of the people who have helped you become who you are. Those who have cared about you, and wanted what was best for you in life." Rogers died in 2002, not long after his retirement from a career of touching so many while doing what he loved.

Knowing that we can be loved exactly as we are gives us all the best opportunity for growing into the healthiest of people. - Fred Rogers

Taite Adams

Realizing Ego Distancing in Wor*

In this section, you'll find seven things to practice in order to make your career speak the language of love, and not that of the ego.

Let Go of the Need to be Right

We learn to be right and to make everyone else wrong. The need to be right is the result of trying to protect the image we want to project to the outside. We have to impose our way of thinking, not just onto other humans, but even upon ourselves. - Don Miguel Ruiz

No matter how smart you are, what position you hold within an organization or even if you work for yourself, if you believe that you hold all of the answers you are destined for failure. According to a study published in the Harvard Business Review, two in five CEOs fail within their first 18 months. One third of chief executives from Fortune 500 companies don't make it past three years. To be a success in any line of work requires a degree of emotional intelligence and this always incorporates some form of humility into the mix.

Do you have a tendency to ignore feedback that you don't agree with or the opinions of people that you don't like in business? To be successful in business, you need to hear the truth, even if you don't like the message or the messenger. If you are only surrounding yourself with "yes people" or people who are going to tell you what you want to hear, you are doing yourself and your organization a disservice. Consider that your ego is driving the bus if you recognize any of these signs:

- You don't have anyone in your inner circle who has a work style or communication style that is unlike your own

- There are rarely challenging viewpoints to decisions that are made

- Your management or leadership team lacks diversity

- Anyone who challenges you is let go as they are seen as not "team players"

Of course, it feels good to be right, at least some of the time. What causes problems is when the overwhelming need to be right dominates you and motivates you to arrange the players in your life as if on a chess board. When you're the person that always has to be right, it turns people off and tunes them out. They no longer hear a word you're saying and will often turn tail and run when they see you coming down the hall.

It's important to realize that just because you're occasionally not "right", it doesn't mean that you're not important or respected. In fact, just the opposite is true. People, and particularly those in business, who are more readily able to admit mistakes or concede a point garner a higher degree of respect among their peers and subordinates. So, how do you let go of the need to be right? It's not as difficult as it may seem. Here are a few suggestions:

- Become a better listener. Stop tuning out or interrupting people who may have different opinions than yours. In fact, welcome the input and genuinely try to understand others points of view.

- Stop being offended. Feeling slighted in the workplace is incredibly common because, for many of us, the stakes are high. Make a concerted effort to stop rolling your eyes, shaking your head, and grumbling whether around others or alone. Learn to accept the things you can't change - which is most everything aside from your thoughts and attitude.

- Be more humble. When you're not right, and even sometimes when you are, be quicker to concede a point and simply move on. People will respect you for this more than you can imagine.

It takes a little bit of mindfulness and a little bit of attention to others to be a good listener, which helps cultivate emotional nurturing and engagement. - Deepak Chopra

Let Go of Your Need to Be Superior

Make it a practice to judge persons and things in the most favorable light at all times and under all circumstances. -Saint Vincent de Paul

When we talk about the need to be superior in business or any other respects, generally this is tied to self-esteem in some form or another, which always goes back to the subconscious ego. Whether we want to spend time blaming our parents for this or not, which is fruitless, the fact of the matter is that if you have a consistent need to be superior to others, you are probably suffering from a low sense of self esteem. Is this always the case? No, not always. Just often enough.

In truth, there are a number of reasons that we put ourselves above other people. One is low self esteem. You don't feel good about yourself on the inside so mask that by putting others down based upon exterior observances. Another form of superiority is exhibiting false pride. This means that you are trying to seem humble or spiritual in order to gain attention and respect. The key here is that you are looking on the outside for validation and that isn't where true fulfillment comes from. I love this simple story about what's important:

A group of graduates from a prestigious university, who were successful and achieving great careers, came to visit their old professor. During the visit the conversation turned to work: The graduates were complaining about countless difficulties and the problems of life.
After offering the guests coffee, the professor went to the kitchen and came back with a coffee pot and a tray, crowded with many different cups: porcelain, glass, plastic and crystalline. Some were simple, others expensive.
When the graduates picked out the cups, professor said:
- Notice, how all the beautiful cups were picked out, and the simple and cheap ones were left. And although it seems normal for you – wanting only best things for

yourself, but that is the source of your problems and stress. You need to understand, that the cup doesn't make the coffee better. Most of the time it's only more expensive, but sometimes it is hiding what we are drinking. Actually, all that you wanted was just coffee, not the cup. But you consciously picked the best cups, and later watched what kind of cups others got.

And now think: life – is coffee, and job, money, position, society – are the cups. They are only instruments for the maintenance and upkeep of life. The type of cup we have, doesn't determine the quality of our life. Sometimes, by concentrating only on the cups, we forget to enjoy the taste of the coffee. The happiest people are not those who have the best things, but those who retrieve everything that is best from what they have.

The need to feel superior to others can manifest itself in many ways, some pretty obvious and some much more subtle. Do you find something wrong with every person you meet or work with? Is everyone an idiot? This is at the extreme end of the spectrum but if you're anywhere near here, it's a virtual guarantee that your attitude is no secret. This isn't going to bode well for a successful business career.

On a more subtle note, do you enjoy gossiping? Think about that moment just before you share a juicy bit of information with someone else and the feeling that you have. It's usually a sense of satisfaction and superiority because you know something that the other person doesn't, whether it be good news or bad. Gossip is about judgment and we already know that this is of the ego.

Letting go of the need to be superior sometimes just requires a bit of perspective. Otherwise, here are some other suggestions:

- Work on your joy. It's a fact that happier people are more kind and considerate to others.

- Know who you are. This sounds a bit misty but it's really what this book is all about. When you are unsure about where you fit in this world, either personally or professionally, you will continue to revert to ego-based behaviors such as acting superior to others.

- Practice forgiveness. Forgiveness isn't just for personal relationships. It should be forefront in all areas of your life, including work. Forgiveness in the workplace can bring forth many benefits that you were previously seeking to gain through manipulation and other non-productive means - things like positive engagement, respect and collaboration.

- Give up the gossip. This is a tough one for many people but once you accomplish it, you'll wonder why you didn't do this years ago. Nothing good comes from gossip. It isn't spiritual in the least and it is engaged in to feed the ego.

Pitting your dream against someone else's is a fantastic way to get discouraged and depressed. - Jon Acuff

Stop Identifying Based on Achievements

What kills a skunk is the publicity it gives itself. - Abraham Lincoln

Funny quote above but what does it mean? Too often our actions and our ways of thinking about the world can turn us into our own worst enemies. This is particularly the case when ego is running the show and you identify yourself in your work setting based on your achievements. For instance, have you ever told yourself, "I'll be happy if I could just get this next promotion", or "So and so is a terrible leader and I should have been given that project"? If you have, you are certainly not alone. But seriously, think of other people that you have worked with that you know identify based only their achievements and the things that they do to "get there". Are they well-like and respected? Probably not.

Negative feelings about external circumstances, including people, at work are all of the ego. When you define yourself based upon achievement - promotions, salary, status, office with a window, parking space, expense account, company car, you get the point - you are throwing up more walls between yourself and other people and fanning the fires of negative emotions such as fear, resentment, anger, and depression. Does this sound like a fulfilling work life? I don't know about you but I've been on both sides of this ego-driven fence and letting go of these sorts of things sure does feel a lot better. So how do we do this?

The key is to understand that happiness in your work is separate from achievement. Don't attach your joy to any certain outcome. When you have this detachment, you will find that you are a much happier person, more relaxed and more yourself. You no longer need to lie and manipulate to get what you want and your fulfillment isn't tied to any one particular outcome. Does this mean that you'll no longer have any achievements and will just now be walking around as a grinning idiot? No, quite the opposite! When you detach from achievement and focus on being happy, honest and the best you that you can be, you are actually more likely to achieve success.

Watch out for the joy-stealers: gossip, criticism, complaining, faultfinding, and a negative, judgmental attitude. - Joyce Meyer

Taite Adams

Let Go of What Others Think About You

We would worry less about what others think of us if we realized how seldom they do. - Ethel Barrett

Have you ever heard the saying, "Dance like no one's watching?" Here's a priceless piece of information for you: No one is. If you are going through life weighing each action and reaction based on what you think other people are going to think, you're feeding into the lie. The truth is that most other people are wasting time thinking exactly the same thing. And that's exactly what it is - a waste of time.

A study done by the National Science Foundation claims that people have an average of 50,000 or more thoughts per day. So, even if a co-worker thinks about you ten times in one day, that's only 0.02% of their overall daily thoughts. It's the unfortunate truth that most people's thoughts are filtered through ego and that means that they are thoughts of self - they relate to "me" or "my". So unless some action that you have taken directly affects them, they are likely not thinking of you at all. This is not a bad thing.

Are there people out there who are still going to judge you? Just as you continue to judge others, you bet there are. This is a fact of life and there are always going to be those few who take unadulterated glee in passing judgment on others. If you become a prisoner to others opinions, you'll never go very far. In fact, the more you stick to your beliefs, the more respected you'll be even by those who don't agree with you.

Worrying too much about what other people think can have a significantly negative impact on your work and career. Some people in this category are seen as pushovers, people-pleasers or just plain annoying. If these are your thought patterns about work, it stands to follow that these are also the same sorts of people that you are going to attract into your life. A group of people-pleasing pushovers isn't conducive to great success.

Here are few ideas to help you let go of what other people think of you in your work:

- Know Thyself. I state this over and over again in this book because it is so critical. It's important that you know who you really are and that you have value just as you are. Once you begin to recognize and embrace this, what others think of you becomes much less important.

- Learn how to say "No". When you know your value and what you believe in, it gives you something to stand up for. You'll also stop being a "Yes" person in order to please everyone.

- Step Outside of Your Comfort Zone. This may need to be baby steps at first but if you are only doing things because you know what the result and the reaction is going to be, you're selling yourself short. In fact, life IS short so the sooner you get out there and start living it the better. When you realize that there is a whole big world waiting out there for you to experience, career-wise included, life becomes much more exciting and vibrant. Take a moment and imagine some of the things that you have cast off because of concern about what other people think. Make a list if it would bring the point home better. Forgoing things that we really want to do in our careers for this reason will only lead to regret. Step outside of your comfort zone and start experiencing life.

Care about what other people think and you will always be their prisoner. - *Lao Tzu*

Be Present

The living moment is everything. - D.H. Lawrence

Have you ever bragged at work about being a great multi-tasker? Many of us have. The truth is that there's no such thing as multi-tasking. You're either present with what is going on at a particular moment or you're not. While it's sometimes fun to play that I'm working on five different things at once, often I'm not getting much done when I do this. It's certainly not quality work. When I focus on what I'm doing, I actually complete the task, do a better job on it, generally get it done faster, and find that I am happier and more satisfied.

A study by Harvard researchers actually shows that a wandering mind is an unhappy mind. In this study, it was found that job satisfaction has a lot to do with focus. So, if you are daydreaming, spending time surfing the net or simply trying to do too many things at once, your lack of focus may lead to unhappiness and eventually to burnout. Is this an ego issue? It certainly can be if you are spending an inordinate amount of your time dwelling on the past or thinking about the future. Staying in the present means that we are focused on what's going on right now. This is where things are getting done, connections are being made and ego distancing happens. Here are some ways to stay present at work:

- Break things down. If you are having a hard time being present or staying focused on a task at work because it just seems so monumental, break it down into smaller, more manageable components. The most important thing is that you do one thing at a time and really experience it.
- Slow down. Life can be hectic. Family, career and other obligations can make scheduling and downtime difficult.

Avoid rushing from one place to the next and take a few quiet moments out for yourself each morning. Don't sleep until the very last minute in the morning so that you are stressed out in traffic all the way to the office. Get the proper amount of sleep (for you) but set your alarm clock a few minutes early so that you have a more relaxing morning routine. If this means that you go to bed earlier at night, so be it.

- Self-care. Aside from the morning quiet time, taking better care of yourself is a must. This will carry through to all areas of your life, including work, and will help you to stay present. Exercise and proper diet are great areas of self-care. So is meditation. These sorts of practices help you to become more self-aware, stay in the present and move you away from ego.

I never think of the future. It comes soon enough. - Albert Einstein

Taite Adams

Be Kind

Be kind, for everyone you meet is fighting a hard battle. - Plato

The workplace is so interesting because we are often thrown into interacting with people that we certainly never would choose to having been given the choice. Have you ever had a difficult boss who treated you like a child? What about a co-worker who made it a habit of stealing other people's work and ideas to further their advancement? These are just a couple of examples of opportunities that we are given in the course of our careers to practice tolerance and just be nice.

But, do we have to be nice to everyone? In a word - Yes. Plato's quote (above) is actually pretty profound when looked at from a personal context. I know that I'm not unkind to others or say mean things unless I am hurting or don't feel good about myself. It's so easy to justify this negative behavior by looking for the fault in others but this process of negativity and then justification is usually done on a subconscious level - and this is ego all the way.

One of the most important things that you can do with regards to kindness is just to become more aware. Notice when you feel the need to be unkind to someone and take a look at what is going on inside of you that is driving those hurt feelings. Once you deal with those feelings in a healthy manner, get back to the business of being kind - to everyone. It doesn't matter if you have a history, good or bad, with someone or if you've just met them. There are always opportunities to be kind. If you're at a loss as to how to begin, here is a fantastic list of 52 ways to show kindness in the workplace:

01. Make a fresh pot of coffee.
02. Clean the microwave (even if it isn't your mess).
03. Smile.

~ 123 ~

04. Say "thank you" in person.
05. Take a co-worker out to lunch.
06. Give a glowing recommendation.
07. Organize a charity drive in your workplace.
08. Organize a volunteer day.
09. Hold the door open for the person behind you.
10. Make a mental list of all the things you enjoy about your work.
11. Be grateful!
12. Be encouraging.
13. Give a compliment.
14. Be constructive in your criticism.
15. Ask someone how they are and really listen to the answer.
16. Introduce a colleague to a contact in your professional network.
17. Be nice to someone you dislike.
18. Be a cheerleader for someone else's idea or project.
19. Tell your boss what you appreciate about them.
20. Make the best of your day.
21. Ask someone for their opinion and consider their position.
22. Invite a co-worker you don't normally socialize with to sit with you at lunch.
23. Share praise with a co-worker's boss and their boss's boss.
24. Let go of a grudge.
25. Take breaks.
26. Give someone else a break.
27. Donate vacation time to a co-worker in need.
28. Share your expertise.
29. Send flowers to a co-worker.
30. Be a mentor.
31. Give someone the benefit of the doubt.
32. Admit when you're in the wrong (it helps other people feel better about their mistakes!)
33. Don't complain.
34. Don't gossip.
35. Share an inspirational quote.
36. Share a uplifting blog post.
37. Tell a joke.
38. Bring in books you loved and pass them on.
39. Be friendly.
40. Forgive someone.

41. Respect others.
42. Say "please" and "thank you".
43. Start and end meetings on time.
44. Learn something new about someone you work with.
45. Bring in fresh fruits or vegetables to share.
46. Give someone a ride to or from work.
47. Pass on coupons you don't need.
48. Start a conversation with the delivery person, janitor, or handyman.
49. Congratulate someone on their accomplishments.
50. Create a custom playlist for a co-worker.
51. Share a positive thought.
52. Be responsible for the energy you bring to your workplace.

Make it your goal to make just a small difference in one person's life each day in your job. We all have the capacity to make a difference. I love the following story that speaks to just that:

I awoke early, as I often did, just before sunrise to walk by the ocean's edge and greet the new day. As I moved through the misty dawn, I focused on a faint, far away motion. I saw a youth, bending and reaching and flailing arms, dancing on the beach, no doubt in celebration of the perfect day soon to begin.

As I approached, I sadly realized that the youth was not dancing to the bay, but rather bending to sift through the debris left by the night's tide, stopping now and then to pick up a starfish and then standing, to heave it back into the sea. I asked the youth the purpose of the effort. "The tide has washed the starfish onto the beach and they cannot return to the sea by themselves," the youth replied. "When the sun rises, they will die, unless I throw them back to the sea."

As the youth explained, I surveyed the vast expanse of beach, stretching in both directions beyond my sight. Starfish littered the shore in numbers beyond calculation. The hopelessness of the youth's plan became clear to me and I countered, "But there are more starfish on this beach than you can ever save before the sun is up. Surely you cannot expect to make a difference."

The youth paused briefly to consider my words, bent to pick up a starfish and threw it as far as possible. Turning to me he simply said, "I made a difference to that one."

I left the boy and went home, deep in thought of what the boy had said. I returned to the beach and spent the rest of the day helping the boy throw starfish in to the sea.

Let no one ever come to you without leaving happier. - Mother Teresa

Gratitude

Do not spoil what you have by desiring what you have not; remember that what you now have was once among the things you only hoped for. - Epicurus

Gratitude is brought up a lot in this book for several reasons. First, when you are "being grateful" for something, you are in the moment and this distances you from ego. Second, when you are in a state of gratitude, your outlook on life changes because gratitude actually has the power to re-wire the brain to see and process the world differently - in a good way.

Unfortunately, work is one of the last places that we think to express gratitude. We don't acknowledge the "goodness" in our work lives and this shows with greater dissatisfaction in our careers. According to a survey of 2,000 Americans released in 2013 by the John Templeton Foundation, people are less likely to express gratitude at work than anyplace else. The survey also indicated that people are not thankful for their present jobs, yet most reported that hearing "thank you" at work made them feel good and motivated. So, we're not grateful for anything yet expect others to express their thanks to us. Astounding.

It's a fact that both saying "thank you" and receiving thanks makes people feel happier and more fulfilled. Yet, we hold back and don't hand out those kudos on the job. In essence, we are robbing ourselves of happiness. Why is this? Some feel that, by expressing any sort of gratitude at work, they would be ripe for the picking and swiftly taken advantage of. Unfortunately, those who don't feel appreciated at work are more likely to just do the bare minimum to get by.

The great thing about gratitude is that it costs nothing and the benefits are enormous. People thrive at work when they know that they are being noticed, appreciated and are making a difference. Not only that, it builds more trust and stronger relationships with the people you work with. As an added benefit, gratitude makes you feel pretty awesome too! People who say thank you are happier, more well-like and more successful. It's one of those cycles that's not vicious at all - it's great!

Here are some tips for showing gratitude at work:

- Be specific and authentic. Don't make a habit of thanking a room full of 50 people for their efforts or, if you do, make sure it's not the only gratitude of the day that you dish out. Gratitude becomes more meaningful when it is personalized to an individual's contribution.

- Check your motives. If you have any ulterior motives for showing gratitude to someone, forget it. Don't do it only in front of your boss so that you'll look good or only for the guy with box seats to tonight's game. Praise should be sincere and without motive for gain or reciprocation.

- Thank people who seldom get thanked. There is a class of employee in nearly every organization that tends to hog all the glory. In hospitals, it's the doctors. In universities, it's the faculty. Take a look around your organization and see if you can identify a few of those "thankless" jobs - the people that aren't getting luncheons and plaques on a regular basis. What about the file clerk, the custodian, the security guard, the cook? If you start thanking these people first, this can set the tone for the entire organization. Check out this short story:

During my second month of nursing school, our professor gave us a pop quiz. I was a conscientious student and had breezed through the questions, until I read the last one: 'What is the first name of the woman who cleans the school?" Surely this was some kind of joke. I had seen the cleaning woman several times. She was tall, dark-

haired and in her 50s, but how would I know her name? I handed in my paper, leaving the last question blank. Before class ended, one student asked if the last question would count toward our quiz grade. Absolutely, said the professor. "In your careers you will meet many people. All are significant. They deserve your attention and care, even if all you do is smile and say hello". I've never forgotten that lesson. I also learned her name was Dorothy.

You are given countless opportunities each day to express gratitude at work. Stop letting them, and your chance at happiness, slip by. When we express gratitude, which is the language of love, we are distancing ourselves from ego and forming bonds with other people. Ego tells us that we are separate from others. Gratitude brings us back together and reminds you that this is a lie.

Silent gratitude isn't much use to anyone. -G.B. Stern

Potential Roadblocks and Solutions

We do not see things as they are, we see things as we are. - Anais Nin

In this section, we just covered seven action items that can help you distance from ego in your work. As with the potential roadblocks in the relationships section, the one's here are very similar as work success often has a lot to do with forming and nurturing relationships. However, if you haven't figured out who you are first, forging strong relationships with other people becomes difficult if not impossible. This brings us back to the emotional intelligence equation once again, where self-awareness is key. There are two things that you need to develop some awareness about in this area of your life: what brings you joy and what fears are holding you back.

It's crucial that you come to some awareness of what brings you joy in your work life. Are you doing the work you love right now? If not, what is that you would rather be doing? If you have absolutely no idea, that's ok and know that you are not alone. One of the things that you will want to do is to start taking some time to discover what you're passionate about. It's not about struggling to get somewhere else. Exactly the opposite. Once you figure out what it is that you truly want, simply allow it to come to you. Doors will open and people will appear where you never expected them to be when you pursue your joy.

So, what's the biggest barrier to realizing our dreams? The one that gets in the way every time as we step out to "pursue our joy"? It's fear, of course. And fear comes from ego. Fear tells you that you're either not going to get something you want or are going to lose something that you already have. So many people live their lives in a state of perpetual fear that it's a wonder many of us find any success at all. So what are we afraid of? Here's just a short list:

- Fear of Failure - This is the most common fear and it can be paralyzing.

- Fear of Success - Many people fear success because they either think they don't deserve it or that they won't be able to sustain it.

- Fear of Change - This is incredibly common. The status quo becomes pretty comfortable and anything else is a move into the unknown. Ego doesn't like the unknown and tells you to be very afraid.

- Fear of Isolation - While ego strives to keep us separate from one another, there is also the very real fear that no one is going to support us wherever we are and that we'll end up "all alone".

- Fear of Not Being Accepted - This is talked about ad infinitum in this book, but it bears repeating. Ego wants us to continuously make comparisons and to never feel good enough. Maybe there is pressure from family or friends to "fit in", or take a certain career path, or that feeling that you're better off just not trying because you'll never be #1.

- Fear of Poverty - Fear of economic insecurity haunts even those who have no reason to fear it. Ego always wants you to view things from a position of lack, rather than from one of abundance.

- Fear of Making the Wrong Decision - Do you see life as one of those complicated mazes where there is only one correct way out and only one "correct" turn at each junction? If so, this can be a crippling fear.

If any of these fears feel familiar to you, you are in good company. I have suffered from many of them at some time or another throughout my life. These sorts of fears can also manifest in all kinds of lovely behaviors that aren't going to help you in your career one bit - things such as: self-sabotage, procrastination, extreme perfectionism, and low self-esteem. That's all well and good but what's more important to note is where these fears came from in the first place. Fear is brought to us by the ego and, more often than not, it's the result of our subconscious playing some tape back over from our past in order to justify why we should be afraid of the present or the future. For instance, I was once promoted to a high-paying management job and the company soon after filed bankruptcy, which left me out of work for a year. Therefore, I should definitely be terrified of any similar promotion opportunities with this present company because a new position with a pay raise will no doubt find me homeless soon after. Makes perfect sense, right?

So how do we overcome these fears that are brought to us courtesy of the ego? Overcoming fears can be another book in itself, yet there are a few things that you can start to re-focus on:

- Change your perception. Remember, thoughts are things and the things that you continually think about are the circumstances that you are going to continue to manifest in your life. Your thoughts influence your feelings, so if you are thinking positive thoughts about any situation, negative feelings have no place in that picture. Therefore, look at each situation and find the positive in it. Focus only on that and move on from there. Emmet Fox advises us to NEVER think about our problems. I wholeheartedly agree with this. If something is bothering you, find something positive to think about or, better yet, think about God instead.

- Banish Self-Doubt. Self-doubt is a dream killer. Don't give voice to it as that makes it grow stronger. It's so important that you believe in yourself because, when you do, others will sense that and believe in you as well. This doesn't mean that you get to walk around being self-deluded that you're going to be the next Michael Jordan if you've never set foot on a basketball court. Instead, formulate an accurate picture of your dreams and your current situation and then set out to make things happen.

- Let go of the outcome. Do you spend an inordinate amount of time daydreaming about the future and some desired outcome? Do you feel better knowing ahead of time what's going to happen? This generally comes from a fear that many of us have that we're not going to be "ok". Remember the exercise that I talked about back in Section I, where I figured out that I had been alive approximately 1.4 Billion seconds? And, during each and every one of those seconds, I've been okay. I haven't always gotten what I wanted but have learned that the things that I want aren't always what's best for me. This is an intelligent universe and your job is to give your best to the present moment, letting go of the outcome, yet knowing that you'll be lead exactly where you need to go and will be taken care of along the way - as you always have been.

There is no illusion greater than fear. - Lao Tzu

Ego Distancing in Health

How Ego Creates Barriers in Health

Modern medicine, for all its advances, knows less than 10 percent of what your body knows instinctively. - *Deepak Chopra*

Health may seem like an odd section to have in a book about ego, but when you consider what we have discussed so far, it should become more clear that someone who is dominated by ego probably isn't pulling the most positive energy into their lives. We'll get into the energy discussion more in a moment, but I want you think about what ego-centered behavior can do to your body. If you spend a lot of time in some of the negative behaviors that we've already talked about at length, chances are you have problems with one or more of the following:

- stomach ulcers
- migraine headaches
- depression and anxiety
- high blood pressure
- heart disease
- drug and alcohol abuse
- sexual dysfunction

I can certainly see myself in this list about 15 years ago. I had many of the disorders and diseases listed here, yet was clueless as to what was really going on in my life. At 30 years old, I was clinically depressed, a drug addict, had terrible stomach ulcers that required hospitalization, suffered frequent debilitating migraines, among many other ailments. I was angry, indignant and a bundle of negative energy. Things just kept getting worse for me - until one day I'd had enough and I changed.

A Body With Healthy Ego Distancing

The physical world, including our bodies, is a response of the observer. We create our bodies as we create the experience of our world. - Deepak Chopra

There is a growing body of evidence that indicates that a person's state of consciousness has everything to do with their energy and their ability to be healed and even to heal others. And energy is the key here as we move into a discussion of health. When I say that I "changed" at the age of 30, that's exactly what I mean. I didn't finally find the right doctor for my ulcers or a miracle drug for my migraines. I changed my consciousness and everything else changed as a result. I stopped the addictive behaviors, the pain went away and a healing energy overtook me. This isn't hocus-pocus stuff. It really works.

The basic idea of quantum physics is that matter is energy. When we talk about energy healing, this is being done at the cell level, which is the result of energy moving to and through a group of cells where some malfunction has taken form. These ideas are discussed in great detail by Dr. Bruce Lipton in his book, *The Biology of Belief*. Dr Lipton brings things one step further wherein he makes the connection between the power of our minds and the actions of our cells. So, if we can send signals to our cells, what would they be? Well, to be disease-free of course! About this, Lipton states:

Endowed with the ability to be self-reflective, the self-conscious mind is extremely powerful. It can observe any programmed behavior we are engaged in, evaluate the behavior, and consciously decide to change the program. We can actively choose how to respond to most environmental signals, and whether we even want to respond at all. The conscious mind's pre-programmed behavior is the foundation of free will.

Deepak Chopra also reflects on many of these same ideas in his book called *Quantum Healing*. As does physicist Amit Goswami, in *The Quantum Doctor: A Physicists Guide to Health and Healing*, where he states that "any physical or emotional difficulty you face has a counterpart in your energy system - and it can be treated at that level."

Is this all just about the power of positive thinking? It only starts there as your thoughts dictate your emotions and then your energy comes from those. However, a change in consciousness is what creates lasting change and achieves ego-distancing. When you are able to do this, you will see benefits that include:

- Increased life span
- Lower rates of depression
- Lower levels of stress
- Greater resistance to disease
- Better physical well-being
- Reduced risk of death from heart disease
- Better coping skills

I can attest to these benefits first-hand. When my consciousness changed, my health and outlook changed 180 degrees. I was no longer depressed, my ulcers disappeared, the migraines went away, I stopped getting sick and I was simply able to cope with life on a daily basis. "Coping with life" sounds too dull. In fact, the colors of life became more vibrant than I ever could have imaged they could be and I started to experience people and places on a whole new level. This is a direct result of a shift in consciousness to a higher energy plane that had a direct and positive result on my health.

Here we're talking about mind-body power that not only can heal you, but that can also harm you. That's some pretty powerful stuff! Most of us have heard of the placebo effect but many don't realize just how powerful this really is. In fact, some historians make an interesting case that the history of medicine is based on this effect. For much of history, physicians had little to use for treatment other than such things as bloodletting, putting arsenic on wounds, and the wide-spread use of rattlesnake oil. Regardless, estimates are that nearly one third of the population is susceptible to the healing "magic" of such treatments.

There are countless studies over the years that show astounding rates of recovery among placebo patients, above and beyond those given the so-called "real" treatments, even surgeries. What studies specifically on the placebo effect tend to agree upon is that its effectiveness rests with the patients "belief" or perception of what they are being given. In other words, if they "believe" they are being cured, many of them are. In fact, there are over 3500 cases of spontaneous remission now documented by the Institute of Noetic Sciences. These are cases wherein the patient was told that they had an incurable, chronic or terminal disease and were able to use mind over medicine to affect a cure.

The placebo effect has incredible implications for self-healing. However, it's shadow - called the Nocebo effect - has some pretty strong potential for self-harm. That same mind-body power that can heal you can also hurt you. When patients in controlled clinical trials were warned about the side-effects they may experience from a drug, nearly 25% of the participants that were taking only sugar pills experienced some severe side effects, including vomiting, memory disturbances, and ringing in the ears. Patients who have been given nothing but saline but thought it was chemotherapy, actually threw up and lost their hair! Again, we're talking about belief! While we may not make the connection, this effect is evidenced over the ages when someone has been told that they are "cursed" to die, be blind, or never bear children and then proceeds to either die, go blind or never reproduce.

So, am I telling you to ditch your doctor, cancel your medical insurance and just start meditating your way to better health? Not at all. What I am suggesting is that you look at your health from a different perspective and take your energy levels into account when it comes to your body. This has everything to do with your thoughts and your beliefs, so take heed those messages that you allow to become a part of your subconscious. Remember that every time a physician tells you that you are suffering from something chronic or incurable, or that you will be on a particular medication for the rest of your life, he is in essence putting a medical hex on you. When you believe these things, and most of us do, they become self-fulfilling prophecies and if you're convinced you're going to die quite soon, you probably will.

Changing consciousness and beliefs is not an overnight matter. There are many things that you can do to work towards this goal and some suggested resources are provided at the end of the book. However, change never happens without positive thinking and positive action, so here are your action items when it comes to ego-distancing and health.

If the structures of the human mind remain unchanged, we will always end up re-creating the same world, the same evils, the same dysfunction. - Eckhart Tolle

Realizing Ego Distancing in Health

In this section, you'll find six things to practice in order to make your health speak the language of love, and not that of the ego.

Let Go of the Need to be Right

Stubborn and ardent clinging to one's opinion is the best proof of stupidity. - Michel De Montaigne

Did you know that stubbornness is considered to be a "dark" personality trait? I can see why it would be called that and I used to be so stubborn that there was no subject open for debate in my book. I had all of the answers already and if they differed with yours, you were dead wrong - end of discussion. Needless to say I was pretty miserable and so was pretty much everyone who came in contact with me. What changed? I did!

The need to be right and the stubbornness attached to it is primarily a resistance to change. We get these ideas about how things are, or should be, from childhood and hold onto them with an iron fist. Many of us would rather fight to the death, and some of us do, rather than succumb to change. But, life is all about change and it's so much easier and enjoyable to simply give up the indignation and go with the flow.

From a health standpoint, nothing says low energy more than a shot of anger and defensiveness towards a fellow human being. When you take the time to get to know yourself more deeply, your mind is going to open and you will begin to look at situations more objectively. I started looking at most things not from a judgment of right or wrong but from a place of love and compassion. When we do this, our ears open to hear other's opinions and we form or deepen relationships based on mutual respect.

It ain't what you don't know that gets you into trouble. It's what you know for sure that just ain't so. - Mark Twain

Taite Adams

Let Go of Your Need to Be Superior

If one does not understand a person, one tends to regard him as a fool. - Carl Jung

I've talked about this in other chapters with regards to relationships and work. However, in this section let's look at letting go of your need to be superior by exercising some humility. As a society, we tend to celebrate over-confidence, entitlement and competitive behavior. Yet, anyone who really takes the time to look within comes to find that these are not the qualities that bring the lasting peace and tranquility that so many of us seek. If you can relate to that old country song "It's hard to be humble, when you're perfect in every way", this is the chapter for you.

One of the virtues that will get you headed in the right direction is humility. Humility is the trait of being unpretentious and not thinking or behaving as if you were better than anyone else. Having humility means that we recognize and accept our limits as well as spend less time being pre-occupied with self. You see that you are but a small, yet important, part in the grand scheme of things, as is everyone else. I love this short, and funny, story on humility that illustrates how we operate under such delusions of grandeur:

A man received a promotion to the position of Vice President of the company he worked for. The promotion went to his head, and for weeks on end he bragged to anyone and everyone that he was now VP. His bragging came to an abrupt halt when his wife, so embarrassed by his behavior, said, "Listen Bob, it's not that big a deal. These days everyone's a vice president. Why they even have a vice president of peas down at the supermarket!" Somewhat deflated, Bob rang the local supermarket to find out if this was true. "Can I speak to the Vice President of peas please?" he asked, to which the reply came: "of fresh or frozen?"

The health benefits from practicing humility are nothing to shake a stick at. Neal Krause, with the University of Michigan, issued findings on his study in 2012 that showed that adults who were more humble rated their health more favorably over a period of time. A study out just this year by psychologist Pelin Kesebir, explains that humility, or a "quiet ego", gives people a more useful perspective on life and their own mortality. It naturally follows that humble people are less stressed. They suffer less fear, anxiety, anger and frustration about life events. Their value isn't dependent upon outperforming others or being the best. When shed of these emotions of resistance, they have lower instances of depression, high blood pressure, and even heart disease.

With humility as something that is desirable from a health standpoint, what's the best way to set out to achieve humility if this is something that has eluded you in the past? Here are a few suggestions:

- Accept and even celebrate your limitations. Not all of us are the best at everything, or even anything. Of course, we all have our unique talents in this world and it's ok to do something well but there is always a limit. Understand this and remember that we are all always learning and improving.

- Recognize your own faults. Instead of looking for and judging the faults of others, recognize that you have your own faults and try to relate to others on that level. Stop judging and start relating and building bridges.

- Look for the positive. Do you ever seek out things to be offended by? Sounds crazy but many of us do this out of habit and this isn't a good one by any stretch. It goes without saying, but I'll say it anyway, that we generally find what we look for and, if you're looking to be offended, even on behalf of others, there's plenty of material out there waiting for you. Stop looking and change your perspective 180 degrees to find what is right with the world.

- Mistakes are beautiful. Don't be afraid to make mistakes or to admit when you have made one. Instead of worrying about being judged for not being perfect, worry only about learning new things and making progress. Admitting mistakes and apologizing when you are wrong will make people respect you like you never dreamed possible.

- Stop bragging. Healthy self-esteem is one thing but constantly bringing attention to your achievements is bragging and unattractive. What's called humblebragging counts too. If you feel compelled to start a sentence with "I don't mean to brag but...", or "You know how much I hate attention but...", it's still bragging. If you do something truly great, chances are it will be noticed without your help.

- Give credit, don't take it. Most of us can look back through our lives and point to key people who gave us help and guidance along the way that helped us to achieve our goals and dreams. Make a point to thank those people for the help that they've given you and don't ever take credit for someone else's accomplishments.

When you get right down to it, most of this book is about humility. When you distance from ego, live in the present moment and re-connect with the Source, peace and humility are what you are going to get. It would also stand to follow that you wouldn't worry so much about what others think of you.

Humility is not thinking less of yourself, it's thinking of yourself less. - C. S. Lewis

Let Go of What Others Think About You

Why should we worry about what others think of us, do we have more confidence in their opinions than we do our own? - Brigham Young

Read through the following list of statements and see if any (or all) of them apply to you:

- I try to be who someone wants me to be.
- I am afraid to rock the boat.
- It is hard for me to know what I want.
- I avoid speaking my mind.
- I find it easier to go along with what someone wants or with their opinion.
- I fantasize about a strong person taking over my life and making it work.
- It is hard for me to express my feelings when they are different from someone I'm close to.
- It is difficult for me to say No.
- I avoid getting angry.
- It is hard for me to take initiative.
- I try to be nice rather than expressing how I really feel.
- I want everyone to get along.

Being constantly worried about what others think of you leads to what is commonly referred to as people pleasing behavior. We want to grace people with our talents, energy and time, encourage them with endless amounts of kindness and have them be forever grateful for our presence. Many people say yes to a plethora of things with the best of intentions, yet don't realize that the underlying motivation is a fear of not being liked or accepted by others. The fear of rejection or fear of failure that is at the root of people pleasing behavior also has some unintended consequences. It's bad for your health.

When you are a chronic people pleaser, saying "yes" for the sake of being liked, accepted or admired, you are doing a disservice to your body and mind in several ways. In essence, by saying "yes" to everyone else, you are oftentimes saying "no" to yourself and neglecting your own health and well-being. Expect to get less sleep and time for personal enjoyment as you are over-committed to a slew of things you probably have no desire to do. Stress and resentment are common amongst people-pleasers, who often resort to using sarcasm as they get bitter over not feeling appreciated. There is also a new study out that points out that people-pleasers are the primary target of bullies. Obesity, alcoholism and addiction can even result as you give yourself up to the whims of the crowd by overeating, over-drinking and taking part in other unhealthy behaviors for the sake of acceptance.

Obviously, if you see yourself in any of these scenarios, change for the sake of your health, well-being and even life itself is in order. I know that, in part, my journey into alcoholism and addiction was due to people pleasing and the need to be accepted. Not surprisingly, this nearly killed me. As happens with addiction, in the end, not only was I not the life of the party - I was all alone. People pleasing behavior is self-sabotage and there are ways to climb out of this pit towards a happier, healthier existence. Here are some strategies to help you stop being a people pleaser:

- Recognize your choices. Many people pleasers really have no idea that they have a choice when someone asks them to do something. I heard many years ago that "No." is a complete sentence and this was profound to me. I don't have to commit to anything - ever.

- Don't give excuses. When you say "No", or "Maybe" to someone's request, you don't have to justify anything or defend your decision. Sometimes when you do this, it gives people room to wiggle in and still try to get you to commit. For instance, as soon as you explain that you can't help on Friday "because you have a new class at the college", someone can come right back at you say, "Oh, that's ok - you can do it on Saturday." Just say "No, I can't do it" and leave it at that.

- Start setting priorities. Often people pleasers don't have priorities because they just try to do everything. This isn't going to happen anymore so take a look at your values and the things that you enjoy and start putting them in order. When you know what is most important to you, this will start becoming much easier.

- Get to the root. The above advice is all well and good but if you don't understand why you have been engaging in these harmful behaviors to begin with, it's going to be difficult to change long-term. Take some time to notice when you are most tempted to do this and what the feelings that come up are. Are they tied to any particular fears? You may wish to journal about it or even seek further counseling.

Bottom line, your self-worth isn't tied to what you do for others or to what others think of you. When you are thinking that it is, this is your ego speaking and the consequences of operating on this low energy plane can be quite severe. Ego distancing through the steps that we've just outlined is one of the surest ways to creating healthy boundaries and, consequently, a healthier you.

A man wrapped up in himself makes a very small bundle. -Benjamin Franklin

Be Present

Be here now. - Ram Dass

Whether you've read the popular book called "Be Here Now" by Ram Dass, "The Power of Now" by Eckhart Tolle, or neither, chances are you've been bombarded by self-help advice touting the importance of being present for your spiritual well-being. While true, and talked about several times already in this book as the practice relates to ego-distancing in relationships and with work, it's also vitally important for your heath. Being present is also currently being used inter-changeably with the word mindfulness, which is a state of active, open attention on the present.

Let's discuss again what being present and mindfulness means and what it doesn't mean. When you are caught up in thinking about the past or the future, you obviously aren't being present. Oftentimes, these are instances where we let our guard down and the subconscious takes over, which is where ego tries to drive us right off the road. You replay old hurts, think about the things you wish you had in your life and make endless irrational judgments. Or, you stress about the future and mentally arrange events so that they turn out the way you want them to.

In light of the above mind games that we allow our ego to play with us by living in a perpetual time warp, it's no wonder that there are health consequences. The most obvious one is stress, depression and anxiety. Lack of restful sleep is another. It's no secret that many people who have recovered from alcohol and drug abuse note an inability to live in the present moment as one of their core issues. High blood pressure, digestive disorders and heart trouble are natural offshoots for those who are in a constant state of regret and remorse about the past or worry about the future.

The damage that we can do to our bodies with our minds is astounding! The healing is also pretty amazing and this is where we come to the health benefits of living in the present and being mindful. To repeat an important point, the present moment is always absolutely perfect. When you are present, you are centered and calm. Stress dissipates as do all of the physical symptoms that tend to follow in its wake, such as blood pressure, sleep issues, gastrointestinal difficulties and even chronic pain.

As further evidence that these aren't pie in the sky claims, new research (2014) from Brown University has uncovered evidence of a convincing link between mindfulness and improved cardiovascular health. Tangible heart-health factors such as blood pressure, obesity and fasting blood glucose were measured against a Mindful Attention Awareness Scale (MAAS). The results showed that people with the highest MAAS scores had an 83 percent higher level of overall cardiovascular health. Being present helps us physically and emotionally on many levels.

For several years now, psychotherapists have been using mindfulness techniques and mindfulness meditation as a key element in the treatment of a number of problems, including: depression, substance abuse, eating disorders, couples' conflicts, anxiety disorders, post-traumatic stress disorder, and obsessive-compulsive disorder. Many experts believe that this works by helping people to accept their experiences rather than react to them with avoidance and aversion.

With so many mind-body-health benefits to being present and mindfulness, the practice is becoming more mainstream. To start reaping the rewards of living in the present moment, here are some tips on practicing mindfulness:

- Awaken to the small things. Start paying more attention to the small experiences of life that you have a tendency to let float past. For example, notice the wind blowing through the trees, the people crossing the street and the vibrant colors of the business signs that you pass. This simple practice brings you back into the moment and can be a good way to notice whether or not you are formulating positive or negative thoughts about these little experiences. If they're not positive, see how you can turn those thoughts around.

- Slow down. Take your world off of auto-pilot and pay more attention to your verbal and non-verbal responses to others. When someone asks you a question or greets you, take the time to slow down, smile and formulate a loving and positive response. This doesn't mean that you give them a "people-pleasing" response, just a kind response that shows you are fully engaged and not just putting them off or placating them.

- Honor your thoughts. Some thoughts that we have zoom through our subconscious, yet we act on them anyway. Make a point of noticing these thoughts as much as possible so that you can begin to understand them better and start to gain some distance from them. For example, if you are having frequent thoughts of "How can I make this person like me?" or "I'm not worthy of success," take notice of these thoughts. Once you recognize them, you can accept them and move on.

- Meditation - Meditation is a big part of being present and practicing mindfulness. There are so many different kinds of meditations out there, that's it's really best if you find one that you are most comfortable with and go with that. There are online live meditation practices, meditation at yoga studios, meditation CDs and even meditation apps for your smart phone. Meditation is so important because it is the best way to connect us to the present moment by focusing on breath and the senses. Check out the resources section at the end of the book for more meditation suggestions.

Bottom line, mindfulness and meditation are good for you. Yes, there is growing evidence to prove this. A recent piece of research by the US National Library of Medicine shows positive health benefits on a group enrolled in a Mindfulness Based Stress Reduction (MBSR) program through the University of Massachusetts Medical School. Participants in the program were found to have denser grey matter after the course, showing more connections and activity in areas related to learning, memory and the capacity to regulate emotion. The study also found an increase in activity in the left side of the brain, associated with positive feelings and emotions as well as a significant boost in the immune system.   The benefits of making a few simple changes are astounding.

Taite Adams

Most people treat the present moment as if it were an obstacle that they need to overcome. Since the present moment is life itself, it is an insane way to live. - Eckhart Tolle

Be Kind

If you haven't any charity in your heart, you have the worst kind of heart trouble. - Bob Hope

In several of the proceeding chapters, we talked at length about kindness. In those sections, we discussed how being kind to others was a key ingredient in ego-distancing and certainly one of the elements in the language of love that brings us back to our Source. If you're not thoroughly convinced that kindness is the way to go, you may be incentivized further by the health benefits. Yes, kindness is actually good for you in the biological sense. What's really amazing about kindness is that it doesn't matter whether you are the giver, the receiver or even an observer of an act of kindness - you still reap benefits to your health.

A Recent Study released by the University of North Carolina found that there may be some connection between kindness and the effect on the vagus nerve:

The vagus regulates how efficiently heart rate changes with breathing and, in general, the greater its tone, the higher the heart-rate variability and the lower the risk for cardiovascular disease and other major killers. It may also play a role in regulating glucose levels and immune responses (...) the vagus is intimately tied to how we connect with one another—it links directly to nerves that tune our ears to human speech, coordinate eye contact and regulate emotional expressions.

In addition to these findings, it's already known that when we perform an act of kindness, our body releases dopamine, a feel-good chemical in the brain responsible for positive thinking. There is also a release of endorphins, those endogenous opioids that are released when we exercise, that also act as a natural feel-good chemical. It has been shown that kindness strengthens immune systems and even increases serotonin levels. All of these medical benefits just from acts of kindness, and no co-pay!

Kindness also gives us healthier hearts. Do you ever get that feeling of emotional warmth after giving, receiving or even witnessing an act of kindness? This is likely the hormone oxytocin that is being released in your brain and throughout your body. Oxytocin causes the release of a chemical called nitric oxide in blood vessels. This expands those blood vessels, which reduces blood pressure. Oxytocin is therefore known as a "cardio-protective" hormone and kindness stimulates its release.

Kindness slows aging! Yes, you read that right. Aging is a combination of many things but our body's deterioration is sped along by two processes: free radicals and inflammation. The same hormone that we just talked about, oxytocin, also reduces free radicals and inflammation in the cardiovascular system and therefore slows aging at its source.

Some people find it easier to be kind than others. Hopefully, you've been given enough incentive to start making this a priority. The payoffs are huge. In the work section, I gave you a list of 52 ways to show kindness in the workplace. The following are another 40 ways that you can show kindness to others.

1. Give up your seat
2. Hold a door open for someone
3. Give a (sincere) compliment
4. Make someone laugh
5. Give someone a hug
6. Take time to really listen to someone
7. Let one car in on every journey
8. Make someone new feel welcome
9. Help someone who's lost
10. Have a conversation with a stranger

11. Pick up litter as you walk
12. Let someone in front of you in the queue
13. Read a story with a child
14. Tell someone they mean a lot to you
15. Let someone have your parking spot
16. Offer your change to someone struggling to find the right amount
17. Treat a loved one to breakfast in bed
18. Buy cakes or fruit for your colleagues
19. Invite your neighbor round for a drink and a chat
20. Offer to help with someone's shopping
21. Tell someone if you notice they're doing a good job
22. Pass on a book you've enjoyed
23. Say sorry (you know who to)
24. Forgive someone for what they've done
25. Visit a sick friend, relative or neighbor
26. Buy an unexpected gift for someone
27. Bake something for a neighbor
28. Pay for someone in the queue behind you
29. Do a chore that you don't normally do
30. Help out someone in need
31. Offer to look after a friend's children
32. Offer to mow your neighbor's lawn
33. Donate your old things to charity
34. Give food to a homeless person and take time to talk with them
35. Visit someone who may be lonely
36. Give blood
37. Get back in contact with someone you've lost touch with
38. Organize a fundraising event
39. Volunteer your time for a charity
40. Plan a street party

Not that you'd still be at a loss, but often kindness is as simple as sitting next to someone when they are sad. This short story illustrates that point pretty well:

A little girl who was late coming home for supper. Her mother made the expected irate parent's demand to know where she had been.

The little girl replied that she had stopped to help Janie, whose bicycle was broken in a fall.

"But you don't know anything about fixing bicycles," her mother responded.

"I know that," the girl said. "I just stopped to help her cry."

What are you waiting for?

Likely the assumption in this section has been that, when we are talking about kindness, we are referring to how we treat others. While that is a big part of it, the way that we treat ourselves is pretty important too and you can derive many of the same benefits that I just listed by showing that same kindness to yourself. If you are continually putting everyone else's needs before your own, and then feeling burnt out and resentful because of it, this is a problem and perhaps you should refer back to the section on Martyrs.

Being kind to ourselves means taking time out for things like self-care, meditation and just plain fun. Just because you are taking care of yourself doesn't mean that you are being ego-centered. If your basic needs aren't met, you're likely going to be a wreck and this leaves you wide open for the subconscious voice of the ego to slip in and start sending those self-serving messages. Therefore, it goes to follow that self care is going to be beneficial for you in many ways. When your needs are met, you are then more open and available to help others. Here are some ideas for self-care:

Taite Adams

- Get enough sleep. When we don't get enough sleep, our moods reflect this. Not only that, so does our health. Immune systems suffer as does mental acuity and mental health. Figure out the proper amount of sleep for your body and mind each night and be sure to set aside the proper amount of time and the right environment for it.

- Exercise. This isn't a physical fitness book but the benefits to the mind, body and spirit of motion are pretty clear. I don't believe that any of us are "unhealthy" or diseased. We all are given the gift of health and some of us are just better at preserving it than others. I know that I did quite a number on my body for many years with drugs and alcohol until I woke up and made a choice to do something different. I choose to honor my body now by not abusing it and by engaging in some exercise as well. These can be gradual changes and done with the help of a professional, yet make a world of difference in your physical and mental well-being.

- Diet. You can take this to the extreme if you'd like by giving up meat, gluten and all other manner of fatty foods, or you can simply start eating a little healthier and add a carrot to your plate every once in a while. I tend to take the latter approach. My dietary regimen was once a complete nightmare, though. Just a few years ago, I lived a pretty sedentary lifestyle and subsisted on sugary sodas, popcorn and crackers. When I decided to make a change and start taking better care of myself, I cut out all of these things and substituted water, dairy products and some fruit. In fact, I eat pretty much anything that I want but don't use food to provide comfort or chase away boredom. This makes a big difference. There are professionals, and a slew of other books, that can help with diet as well.

- Have fun. I can't stress enough how much taking time out for the things that you enjoy is key to your own self-care and growth. This is absolutely different for everyone so I certainly can't tell you what to do. Regardless, if you don't know what to do - experiment!   Spend time in nature, volunteer with children, learn to paint - ask others for ideas. I know that one of the things that I enjoy most is reading. There were many years that I couldn't do this because I simply wasn't mentally or emotionally capable of being present enough to read a book and follow a story. Now I am and I absolutely devour books of all sorts. This is one of my joys and a way that I take care of myself daily - now go find yours!

Be sure to incorporate kindness to others and self-care into your life, along with keeping a keen eye on appreciation and gratitude.

The way you think, the way you behave, the way you eat, can influence your life by 30 to 50 years. - Deepak Chopra

Gratitude

God gave you a gift of 86,400 seconds today. Have you used one to say "thank you? -William A. Ward

So far, every section of this book has had a chapter on Gratitude. There is a very good reason for this and I believe that living in a state of appreciation for all that life has to offer is one of the surest ways to distance ourselves from ego. When you are grateful for everything that you have, including all of your past experiences, what could there possibly be to judge or complain about? And, isn't that what ego loves to do the most? It was mentioned briefly much earlier but it must be emphasized here that gratitude has an added benefit - it makes you healthier.

One of the foremost researchers on gratitude is Dr. Robert Emmons, a psychology professor at the University of California at Davis. He studies in a growing field called "positive psychology" and has found through his research that those who have an "attitude of gratitude" as a permanent state of mind experience many health benefits. Specifically, people who are grateful are more likely to:

- Take better care of themselves physically and mentally
- Engage in more protective health behaviors and maintenance
- Get more regular exercise
- Eat a healthier diet
- Have improved mental alertness
- Schedule regular physical examinations with their doctor
- Cope better with stress and daily challenges
- Feel happier and more optimistic
- Avoid problematic physical symptoms
- Have stronger immune systems
- Maintain a brighter view of the future

Of course, looking that list, gratitude is starting to look a lot more attractive from a health and wellness standpoint. Remember, Emmons called this an "attitude of gratitude" and attitude plays a key role here. Gratitude is all about how you view both the outside world and yourself. If you are able to see more of the positives in your life, despite any existing challenges, consider yourself grateful.

Gratitude really has nothing to with material possessions, or lack thereof. This is a misconception many have - that those who have the most "stuff" have more to be grateful for. This isn't true at all and there is even research to back this up. Dr. Edward Diener, a psychology professor at the University of Illinois, concluded that a high percentage of affluent people in Japan report low levels of life satisfaction, similar to those living in poverty in India. This suggests that it's not how much you have, but how you feel about what you have that really matters.

If you would like to increase the level of gratitude in your life and start reaping the benefit listed above, here are some suggestions to get started:

- Keep a gratitude journal. This is a great strategy and very effective for increasing your level of appreciation. There are quite a few of these on the market and some even have lists of "suggestions" should you not be able to come up with anything to be grateful for on a particular day. Pick a consistent time each day to sit down with your journal and list about three to five things that you are grateful for. This gets you into the daily practice of paying attention to what is going well in your life and just how much you really are blessed.

- Have a gratitude partner. Engaging someone else in our journey is one way to bring extra discipline and commitment to the equation. Several people working together to encourage healthy behaviors is a great way to develop new habits and gratitude partners have an added benefit. I actually have several gratitude partners and we share with each other each day at least one thing that we're grateful for. Often, the things that other people are grateful for are things that had never crossed my mind that I should, or could, be grateful for and there's the added gift.

- Change your self-talk. This often happens naturally as you continue the gratitude exercises over a period of time, but many people's inner-dialogue isn't positive by nature. Research shows that we can change our mood by changing the tone of the things we are saying to ourselves. Practice re-framing any situation that you see as a challenge into something positive. This isn't rocket science - it's a simple mental exercise. Find the positive in every situation and be grateful for it.

There is just no getting around that turning bad things into good things is up to you. - Deepak Chopra

Taite Adams

Potential Roadblocks and Solutions

Fear seems to have many causes. Fear of loss, fear of failure, fear of being hurt, and so on, but ultimately all fear is the ego's fear of death, of annihilation. To the ego, death is always just around the corner. In this mind-identified state, fear of death affects every aspect of your life. - Eckhart Tolle

In Part I of this book, I talked a lot about what the ego is and how we define ourselves. Whether you define yourself by your name, your occupation, your possessions and achievements, there is one thing that is certain - you are defining a finite self that is destined at some point to die. Your ego is either screaming in your ear that you should be very afraid of this inevitability or that you should ignore it completely because this is going to happen to everyone but you. Of course, neither scenario is true and our attitudes about death are the biggest roadblock to ego distancing in health.

And this is where we begin to speak even more of God. Anyone who has distanced from ego enough has undoubtedly experienced the infinite power of God, or the Source if you prefer. God is universal, which means that He is everywhere, at all times. In other words, infinite. As we are all made in His image, it would follow that we are infinite beings as well. By taking a page from Buddhism, death is not the end of life but merely the end of the body that we inhabit in this life. Our spirit still remains, only to be re-born at some point. Death is still important in Buddhism, however, because the awareness of death is what prompted the Buddha to see and understand the ultimate futility of worldly goods and pleasures. The most important thing that the Buddhists focus on is their mental and spiritual development because that is all that is taken with them to the next life.

E-Go

While we all may have an appointment with destiny, what most of us don't realize is that your number is being called right now! Life is eternal, infinite and all-inclusive. There is no need to wait for life to begin or for it to end. The magic is happening in this very moment. When you live in a state of gratitude and amazement for everything that has been placed in your path, you'll be able to quickly turn any challenge into a blessing. The Source is handing you unlimited potential for all that you desire and fear of becoming sick or dying will simply hold you back from this abundance. If these are stifling fears that are pulling you away from a healthy and happy life, consider these suggestions:

- Remember that God didn't create anything finite. Love is the opposite of fear. Love is of God and love is eternal. You are also of God, are a loving soul and are eternal.

- Your appointment is now. You don't have to live a life waiting "for the other shoe to drop", wondering when you're going to get sick or when you're going to die. Your infinite and perfect life is happening right now and you can start living it at any time you choose.

- Reposition negative thoughts. It's okay to still get fearful, apprehensive and even angry sometimes. When you do, become mindful of the feelings, recognize that they are coming from ego and reposition those thoughts to positive thoughts and feelings of gratitude.

He who doesn't fear death only dies once. ~Giovanni Falcone

Part III - We Are All One

The Universal Source

The only intelligent question is what kind of God do you believe in, because everybody believes in some God, even those who do not like the word. - Emmet Fox

Ego-based thinking is based on a belief of separation. We believe that we are separate from each other and from the Universal Source. Do you believe that you are an isolated entity in this universe? Before you answer that question, or allow your ego to answer it for you, let's look at what an isolated system is. A system that is isolated implies that there is no interaction with other systems in its environment. Hint: there are no isolated systems found in nature - anywhere. Tibetan Buddhists teach this as do countless other traditions throughout the world.

As human beings, we attempt to define our outlines by our physical bodies, but this is another false assumption. The finite self is an illusion as the energy that we are made up of is infinite. This isn't guru-talk - it's been scientifically studied by the likes of Einstein, among others, in his Unified Field theory, which attempts to correct our concepts of the world as a closed system. This theory was the basis for String Theory, sometimes also referred to as the "theory of everything" or TOE, which proclaims that particles in the universe that compose matter can be reduced down to an infinite vibrating "string", thus never-ending and all connected. String Theory also claims that there are many dimensions to the universe and that, as human beings, we are only able to relate on four of them which represent space and time.

However, infinity is a part of this theory as is the idea that we are all connected through our Creator and through our consciousness.

So, how does this relate to ego distancing and what we have been talking about in this book? It has everything to do with it because your ego wants you to believe that you are the all-powerful force in the universe that must make everything happen and see that everyone else behaves. As long as you continue to believe this, you will remain unhappy and will continue to look for more books about how to find peace and happiness. Looking for fulfillment in external conditions is a tiresome and fruitless exercise. Whether your ego is getting in the way of your relationships, work or your health, more than likely you have a nice combo plate going, it all comes down to false ideas about self and believing that you are a separate entity in this world. Nothing could be further from the truth.

Whether you dislike the word "God" or not, there are many alternatives on hand that serve just as beautifully - Divine Source, Universal Intelligence, Universal Mind or Higher Power. It really is hard to argue that there is a higher intelligence operating in the universe, that some call God's plan. Taoists call this universal intelligence the Tao, or the Way of Nature. Some other traditions speak of a cosmic consciousness. Whether religious, spiritual, or even scientific, there has been much consensus across disciplines that there is something ultimately mysterious and creative about the order of the universe.

The fact that the universe is tuned so precisely and in such a way as to allow the possibility of human life should give anyone pause. There are volumes of works that discuss in detail just how perfect the order of our universe really is, so I won't spend pages on it here. But consider the precision of our solar system that allows life on earth, the make-up of our planet itself, the order and design seen in the animal world, the precision of our oceans, and the order of the human body itself.

Universes are complex, law-governed entities and there must be some underlying, unifying cause of their creation and continuing existence - or some sort of "God".

The harmony of natural law...reveals an intelligence of such superiority that, compared with it, all the systematic thinking and acting of human beings is an utterly insignificant reflection. - Albert Einstein

Taite Adams

We Are Part of God

I am part or particle of God. - Ralph Waldo Emerson

Remember, one of the main things that our ego wants us to believe is that we are separate from God, what's sometimes referred to as Separation Theology. Considering the things that we've just covered about this divine, intelligent universe that we live in, how can this be so? It's actually not. If it's not true that we are separate entities from the Universal Source, then how could we suffer from "not having God?" The answer is that we are not suffering from the "fact" that God is not here with us, rather from the belief that he isn't. While you may believe in one thing or another as much as you wish, there's no doubt that the pain you suffer from your choices is very real.

Anyone who went to bible school as a child was probably taught that we were all made in the image of God. Many of us as children took this literally but what this really means is that we all have the spark of the infinite Creator within us. In fact, the idea that we are all a part of God is a founding truth behind many of the world's great faiths. While there are different terms and labels used to describe God within various religions, with study it soon becomes evident that some of the spiritual greats of history - Jesus, Buddha, Muhammad - believed that God lies within each person.

"Is it not written in your law, 'I have said you are gods' " - Psalms 82:6

'Man is mystery and I am his mystery, for I am he himself and he is I myself.' - Muhammad

If God resides in each of us, what then are the implications for you right now and for your ego? Great news! This means that you no

~ 177 ~

longer have to "hope" for something better, have to fight for your fair share, need to compare against and judge others because divine perfection is with you right here and now. Heaven itself is a state of mind, a consciousness, that is available right here in this moment to anyone who chooses it. Those who are tuned in to this level of consciousness have moved the furthest away from ego and tend to be operating at very high energy levels. Those who recognize their oneness with both the Universal Source and with all of life, move even further.

Someday, after mastering the winds, the waves, the tides and gravity, we shall harness for God the energies of love, and then, for a second time in the history of the world, man will have discovered fire. - Pierre Teilhard de Chardin

We Are All One

There are no extra pieces in the universe. Everyone is here because he or she has a place to fill, and every piece must fit itself into the big jigsaw puzzle. - Deepak Chopra

The final reason given for ego-centered beliefs was the idea that we are separate from each other. In the previous chapter, I talked about the Separation Theology, wherein we believe we are separate from God. If we can replace this with a Oneness Theology, ego-distancing is a sure thing. By recognizing that not only are we a part of God, but also that we are one with all of life, Heaven's doors really do open up and the language of love will become your new mantra.

Why is this so difficult for some to accept? The most common reason is because we believe our individuality proves that we are separate and, oftentimes, alone.

We are so not alone, however. The wholeness of the universe defines its parts. English mathematician and philosopher Alfred North Whitehead was a leader in 20th century process philosophy, which stresses God's relational nature. Whitehead remarks, "The misconception which has haunted philosophic literature throughout the centuries is the notion of independent existence. There is no such mode of existence. Every entity is only to be understood in terms of the way in which it is interwoven with the rest of the universe." Human beings are not distinct from nature or from each other in such a world. As star dust, we have grown out of this cosmos and are inseparable from all that is, including each other.

For those who still wish to claim separateness, that's ok. I can be pretty stubborn at times too. There is some evidence out there showing some pretty radical connections between the thoughts of human beings across fields of energy. It's a phenomenon called the "multiples effect" and is said to occur when multiple people who are isolated from each other geographically come up with the exact same discovery simultaneously. By 1922, there had been 148 major scientific breakthroughs identified to have been discovered in this way. Here are a few of the examples:

- Evolution (Darwin and Wallace)
- Calculus (Newton and Leibniz)
- Decimal fractions – 3 people
- Sunspots – 4 people in 1611
- Law of conservation of energy – 4 people in 1847
- Steamboat – 4 people
- Telescope – 9 people
- Thermometer – 6 people

Possibly a few of these could be chalked up to coincidence but you'd be hard-pressed to contribute the law of chance to this many instances. What this tells us is that there were likely several people working on a problem, say sunspots, as the same time and interacting with each other across a field of energy that knows no physical boundaries. There is a connection there that has nothing to do with geography and everything to do with consciousness.

The consciousness that I refer to is the One Mind of this universe, or the vast sea of energy that vibrates at one speed or another. You play a great role in this consciousness by how you communicate within it. The language of these energy vibrations comes from our feelings and emotions. This is where you make your choices. You can operate in this universe at very low levels of energy, and attract the same sorts of people and situations, by radiating negative feelings of anger, resentment, judgment, and lack. Or, you can exist in the higher energy planes of consciousness by radiating feelings of joy, compassion, forgiveness and love.

To believe that our choices and energy levels only affect us, is fallacy and contrary to what this book is all about. Of course our energy, negative or positive, has a direct affect on those around us but it has also been shown that we have the power to influence things on a much grander scale - just by changing our thoughts. Imagine creating global change through positive emotions!

The Japanese author Masaru Emoto has documented some interesting experiences regarding positive thinking and water droplets. He says that if human speech or thoughts are directed at water droplets before they are frozen, images of the resulting water crystals will be beautiful or ugly depending upon whether the words or thoughts were positive or negative. Mr. Emoto and colleagues have done experiments with water and how it will be affected in its frozen formation. They have looked at environmental conditions, pollution, music and even thoughts and words. The pictures on the next page show the formation of untreated, distilled, water crystals, using words typed onto paper by a word processor and taped on glass bottles overnight.

Water is the mirror that has the ability to show us what we cannot see. It is a blueprint for our reality, which can change with a single, positive thought. All it takes is faith, if you're open to it. - Masaru Emoto

Considering that about 71% of the Earth's surface is water-covered, and the human body is more than 60% water, implications that we have control over its structure through our consciousness are pretty significant. Emoto's work and findings on consciousness has influenced millions, and paved the way for a massive transformation in the evolution of consciousness, quantum physics, and our understanding of reality.

With all of this evidence that we are connected through our consciousness by energy, water, and other means it becomes impossible to exist any longer as an island and to continue to give credence to the negative and untrue thoughts that ego sends - you are all alone, you deserve more than someone else, people don't appreciate you enough, you have to behave a certain way to be liked and accepted, and so on.

Letting go of these old ideas and practicing the action items that have been outlined in this book are the things that are going to get you the furthest distance from ego.   When you start taking action on these items, you'll find that voice getting quieter, more distant, because you will find that you have begun to speak the language of love.

We are here to awaken from the illusion of our separateness. - Thich Nhat Hanh

Taite Adams

The Language of Love

Love is the crowning grace of humanity, the holiest right of the soul, the golden link which binds us to duty and truth, the redeeming principle that chiefly reconciles the heart to life, and is prophetic of eternal good. - Petrarch

In one of the beginning chapters, I talked about how ego's opposite was Love. The sections on ego distancing in relationships, work and health tell us how to do achieve this through various measures and action items. To come to a place of knowing that we are not separate from each other and separate from God is the biggest leap that you can take in distancing from ego.

The Bible tells us that "God is Love" (1 John 4:8). If we are also a part of God, then we are essentially beings of Love as well. God's love is unconditional and so must be ours, which means that forgiveness isn't something that is just handed over to those we deem worthy on special occasions. Profoundly, Lily Tomlin once asked, "If love is the answer, could you please repeat the question?" The question being put to you right now is whether or not you wish to be happy, prosperous and at peace in your life? If this is what you would like, the answer is love.

By operating from a place of love in your life, in everything you do, you are doing many things that will distance you from ego and bring you to a life beyond your wildest dreams. Cooperating with a Universal Source, rather than working against it in all of your endeavors, requires a true sense of humility. You will begin to see your place in this world as a part of a great whole, no longer making distinctions or judgments that place you in a position of superiority or a need for approval. You begin to appreciate and enjoy the differences between people, rather than seeing them as something to judge or dislike because we are all spiritual beings and all connected.

Because we are all connected, you will become much more in tune to the signals that the universe is sending you, including people and situations. Some may be lessons to learn but many are people and situations perfectly designed to help you move on to a new level of consciousness and achievement towards the things that you desire. You'll begin to see the value of "letting go" of control of the outcome of situations and simply doing your best job to influence whatever is in your control at a particular moment in time. When you speak the language of love you know that your joy isn't contingent upon anything external to yourself. It is within you and has been all along.

With regards to time, the present moment will become the most precious because you will suddenly realize that the "Now" is where all of the joy in life resides. It does not exist in reliving the past or daydreaming and fretting about future events that may never come to pass. Heaven exists right in the here and now and you are given a moment to moment choice as to where you wish to reside. Ego doesn't want you to live in the present moment and be mindful of your thoughts and emotions. As soon as you stop, take note of your breath, the wind flowing through the trees and fragrant smell of the candle burning in the room, you've won a victory.

There is no love in this life if we continue to be only concerned with self. Universal Intelligence is just that - Universal. It is concerned with the well-being of the whole, not just little old me. So, if you open yourself up to the power of Universal Intelligence, you are opening yourself up to the Whole. If you continue to operate on a level that benefits self at the expense of someone or something else, it's not going to go as planned. Conversely, if you work for the benefit of the Whole, you will benefit more than you could have ever dreamed. Being kind and helping others is a must.

When you speak and live the language of love, gratitude is a foregone conclusion. You are able to find something positive in every situation, even those that seem like obstacles on the surface. Life's lessons are there to bring you to new levels of consciousness and to help you operate at higher energy vibrations. This brings more positive situations and people into your life in a never-ending cycle of growth. Finding fault in situations and in people is futile because we are all a part of a Divine whole and a perfect plan. Nature is something to be exalted as is each encounter you have with another person on this journey.

Feeling bad and living fear is an absolute choice. If you are speaking the language of love, you know that you are in Heaven regardless of what is going on around you at any particular point in time. You learn how to use your emotions and thoughts as a barometer that it's time to make a conscious change in thought to love. Being offended no longer something you choose to do. Low energy people do exist in this world, in some places more than others, but you don't need to dominate or even be around these people to continue to feel and spread your love.

Fear is of the ego, plain and simple. It is also the antithesis of love. We cannot be in fear and love at the same time, so it is a choice. As human beings, we have the gift of conscious awareness, of which we are able to direct through our choices. This isn't about judging ourselves at all - the idea is to stop judging altogether and have compassion and love for all of creation. This includes you. Treat yourself right, know your value, recognize your unity with the universe, be kind, say "thank you", and you will find the ego distancing that you so desire - and so much more.

Resources

Assistance and Methods for Changing Consciousness

This book frequently makes reference to the ideas that are formed into our subconscious as being the basis of ego behavior. As most of these ideas are formed at an early age and are deeply implanted, they can be difficult to both identify for what they really are and then to make any lasting changes on both a conscious and subconscious level. While the action items listed and described throughout the book will go a long way towards ego distancing, to really reprogram the subconscious requires a true examination and change of old idea to new, more healthy ones. Here are some resources that may be able to help you in that regard:

12 Step Programs (http://en.wikipedia.org/wiki/Twelve-step_program) - Those who view 12 Step Programs as trite or as something only for alcoholics or addicts are shaking a proverbial stick at a proven method for a program that delivers nothing less than a total personality transformation in those that apply its principles to their lives. Strongly influenced by Jungian therapy, the 12 Steps provide a spiritual remedy to any number of issues through surrender of the ego and the examination of old ideas. With the Steps being adapted to over 200 self-help organizations, the results in individuals from their application is a miraculous change in consciousness unattainable from other methods. I highly recommend anyone seek out a program that fits their particular issue and jump in. There is never a monetary investment required, which cannot be said for many of the other programs listed here.

Alchemical Healing (www.shamanicjourneys.com) - Alchemical Healing combines innovative methods from shamanism and energetic healing with the principles of alchemy to create physical healing, therapeutic counseling, and spiritual growth.

The Body Code System of Natural Healing (www.drbradleynelson.com) - The Body Code System for Ultimate Energy Healing and Body Balancing is a program to find and correct underlying imbalances that block health and happiness.

Body Talk System (www.bodytalksystem.com) - BodyTalk is designed to resynchronize the body's energy systems so they can operate as nature intended.

Core Health (http://corehealth.us) - Core Health's DTQ (Deeply, Thoroughly, Quickly) is a process to permanently reactivate a person's innate healthy core.

EMDR (www.emdr.com) - EMDR is a psychotherapy that enables people to heal more quickly than traditional therapy from the symptoms of emotional distress that result from disturbing life experiences.

Emotional Freedom Techniques (www.eftfree.net) - Based on new discoveries about the body's subtle energies, Emotional Freedom Techniques are used as therapy for emotional, health, and performance issues.

The Hendricks Institute (www.hendricks.com) - The Hendricks Institute is an international learning center that teaches core skills for conscious living and conscious loving and is committed to creating a world-wide community of people who want to explore new heights of love, creativity, and well-being.

Holographic Repatterning (http://repatterning.org) - Resonance Repatterning is a system to identify and clear the patterns of energy underlying any issue, problem, or pain you are experiencing.

Inner Resonance Technologies (http://innerresonance.com) - Inner Resonance features seven steps designed to allow each person's automatic system to rebalance and harmonize physically, emotionally, mentally, and spiritually.

The Journey (www.thejourney.com) - The Journey is designed to access the body's own healing wisdom at the deepest level of "source" or the soul.

NetMindBody (www.netmindbody.com) - NetMindBody is a mind-body stress-reduction process for finding and removing neurological imbalances related to unresolved mind-body issues.

PSYCH-K (www.psych-k.com) - PSYCH-K is a set of principles and processes to change subconscious beliefs that limit the expression of your full potential as a divine being that is having a human experience.

Rapid Eye Technology (http://rapideyetechnology.com) - Rapid Eye Technology releases stress and trauma by stimulating REM sleep, your body's own natural release system.

Reconnective Healing (www.thereconnection.com) - Reconnective Healing uses vibrational frequencies to heal body, mind, and spirit.

The RIM Method (http://riminstitute.com) - The RIM Method reconstructs affirming images in cellular memory to create subconscious changes for accelerated emotional and physical well-being and greater success.

The Sedona Method (http://www.sedona.com) - The Sedona Method teaches people how to tap into their natural ability to release painful or unwanted feelings, beliefs, and thoughts.

Silva UltraMind ESP System (http://silvaultramindsystems.com) - The Silva UltraMind ESP is a system to unlock the incredible powers of people's minds to connect to a higher power that provides guidance for leading a happier and more successful life.

Three in One Concepts (http://3in1concepts.us) - Based on research and development in the field of applied kinesiology, Three in One Concepts assists people who want to take responsibility for creating their own well-being by integrating body, mind, and spirit.

The WOW Process (http://thewowprocess.com) - WOW is a process to alleviate physical, emotional, or spiritual stress and suffering.

Meditation Resources

Basic meditation with Tara Brach (http://www.tarabrach.com/audioarchives-guided-meditations.html) - Free meditations that you can stream or download.

Breathworks (www.breathworks-mindfulness.org.uk) - Meditation and pain management

Chopra Center Meditation (http://chopracentermeditation.com) - Download and listen to mediations from Deepak Chopra.

Clear Vision: (www.clear-vision.org) - Online resources for meditation (and Buddhism) for young people and schools.

Contemplative Mind in Society
(www.contemplativemind.org/practices/recordings)
Guided practices from Mirabai Bush, the center's director, Diana
Winston from UCLA's Mindfulness Awareness Research Center, and
Arthur Zajonc, president of the Mind & Life Institute.

Dharmacrafts Learning Resources
(www.dharmacrafts.com/100xRS/Learning-Resources.html)

Free guided meditations from UCLA
(http://marc.ucla.edu/body.cfm?id=107)
Each week has a different theme, and usually includes some
introductory comments, a guided meditation, some silent practice time,
and closing comments. Presented by the UCLA Mindful Awareness
Research Center.

Holosync (www.centerpointe.com) - Holosync is a form of
neuroaudio technology for creating a balance between brain
hemispheres to enhance mental/emotional health and mental
functioning.

Insight Meditation Society
(www.dharma.org/resources/audio#guided)
Selected talks, podcasts, and audio streams, including various lengths
of guided meditation.

LifeFlow Meditation (www.project-meditation.org) - Based on
biofeedback research, LifeFlow Meditation places the listener into
brain-wave states that enhance happiness, well-being, and learning
abilities.

Omvana (www.omvana.com) - Claimed to be the world's #1 meditation app in over 30 countries, this mobile app makes customizing your meditation experience fun and easy. This app contains thousands of audio tracks, beats, and sounds that you can blend together in the app's mixing board. If a stranger's voice is unsettling, you can even record your own voice and use it to guide your meditation sessions instead.

The Metta Foundation (http://metta.org) - "It is the mission of the Metta Foundation to foster the convergence of wisdom born of traditional meditative stillness and compassion born of human encounter."

The Mindfulness App (www.mindapps.se) - Available on iphone and Android, this meditation app is straightforward and simple. Guided meditation sessions can span from 3 to 30 minutes.

Vipassana meditation website (www.dhamma.org) - One of the most widespread forms of meditation practice.

World Wide Online Meditation Center (www.meditationcenter.com) - A user-friendly site, created to provide clear, straight-forward meditation instruction to people anywhere on the planet.

Gratitude Resources

365 Grateful (http://365grateful.com) - A personal quest to be happier became a gratitude movement and is now a documentary in the works—see the astounding evolution of one woman's simple practice of being grateful.

Gratitude Log. (www.gratitudelog.com) - Bills itself as the happiest place on the Internet where you can connect with other grateful people.

Greater Good: The Science of a Meaningful Life. (http://greatergood.berkeley.edu) - This University of California, Berkeley site is full of great articles about gratitude and positive approaches to life. Sign up for the 14-day gratitude challenge and see if it makes a difference in your life.

Templeton Foundation (www.templeton.org) - A foundation dedicated to focusing the methods and resources of scientific inquiry on the moral and spiritual dimensions of life.

Unstuck: A Practical Guide to Gratitude. (www.unstuck.com/gratitude.html) - Learn 9 ways to cultivate gratitude and discover the power of paying a compliment.

Spirituality Resources

Beliefnet.com (www.beliefnet.com) - One of the most wide-ranging spirituality websites on the internet, Beliefnet claims that they have "something for everyone" and they really do. The site offers everything from articles on all the major world religions to daily tips for health and happiness.

DailyOM.com (http://dailyom.com) - DailyOM is a spiritual home away from home for many believers and seekers. The site name is very appropriate because it really is the sort of site you visit every day. DailyOM is perfect for social networking with spiritually aware and like minded folks.

ElephantJournal.com (www.elephantjournal.com) - Waylon Lewis, the founder of *Elephant Journal* calls himself a "mediocre, lazy yogi" and a "1st generation American Buddhist" but he is also a multi award winning media hero who is helping to change the world for the better.

HighExistence.com (www.highexistence.com) - HighExistence (HE) is a community of conscious individuals centered around pondering, exploring & expanding this wondrous experience called life. The mission of the site is compel you to follow your bliss; make a life, not a career; and question anything and everything that is considered 'normal'!

Institute of Noetic Sciences - IONS (http://noetic.org) - "Noetic" comes from the Greek word nous, which means "intuitive mind" or "inner knowing." The institute researches consciousness with the hope of transforming the world. The section dedicated to intuition, parapsychology and subtle energies are very interesting.

Taite Adams

About the Author

Taite Adams grew up everywhere. The only child of an Air Force navigator and school teacher, moving around became second nature by grade school. By age 20, she was an alcoholic, drug addict and self-proclaimed egomaniac. Pain is a great motivator, as is jail, and she eventually got sober has found peace and joy in this life beyond measure.

At the age of 42, Taite published her first book titled "Kickstart Your Recovery". Now permanently Free on Amazon, the book answers many of the questions that she herself had but was afraid to ask before giving up the fight with addiction and entering recovery over a decade prior. Since, she has published four other recovery books, including her bestselling book on Opiate Addiction, and has moved into the broader spirituality and self-help genres.

Leading a spiritual life is all about choices. The practice of spiritual principles and the willingness to remain teachable are the key ingredients for growth. As a spiritual seeker and reader of the self-help genre herself, Taite appreciates and respects each and every person who takes the time to read her works and respond with reviews and comments. For more information on books, upcoming releases, and to connect with the author, go to http://www.taiteadams.com.

Check out our active Facebook Page: Taite Adams Recovery Books (facebook.com/TaiteAdams).

As you begin your Road to Recovery, please check out Taite's first book, **Kickstart Your Recovery**, available in both Kindle (where's it is Permanently FREE) and Paperback.

Opiate Addiction has reached epidemic proportions in this country and is something that Taite is intimately familiar with. Read her bestselling book on this topic, chronicling this insidious killer and laying the pathway for freedom from its grip.

Should you require additional assistance with your home detox, be sure to pick up Taite's popular book, *Safely Detox From Alcohol and Drugs at Home*, also on Amazon.com.

If you or a loved one are in recovery from alcoholism or addiction and want to learn more about emotional sobriety, check out Taite's book titled *Restart Your Recovery*, also on Amazon.com.

It's hard to miss mention in the media of the drug Molly and the controversy surrounding it's use and it's ingredients. There is plenty of confusion there as well. Check out Taite's latest book, called *Who is Molly?* for the latest info on this drug and it's dangers.

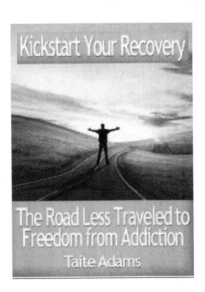

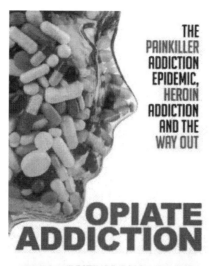

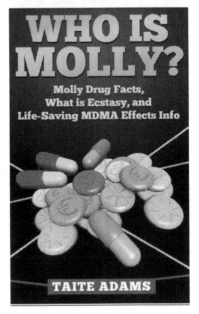

Taite Adams